Your Brain

Your friend or your enemy?

Damian Podpora, 2024

Yesterday, falling asleep, I listened to the audiobook "Kwantechizm 2.0", a book on quantum physics by a brilliant Polish physicist, Andrzej Dragan. I like to listen to boring books in bed, because then I fall asleep faster, but unfortunately for me – this book turned out to be hellishly interesting. Voice narrator was reading something about black holes, and at some point I thought:

"There are holes somewhere in space. Funny."

You know, it's a bit strange when we seriously think about it... Imagine that suddenly, a voracious hole appears in your room that absorbs everything, like Aunt Christine, who, after two weeks of a cabbage diet, throws herself on a tray of apple pie and absorbs it in five minutes. Well, just close your eyes and think – how can a hole appear in the world? Our world isn't some fucking piece of cheese, is it?

And yet such holes exist. And it's not theory, it's not Science Fiction, it's not even nonsense. That's true. The world has millions (or maybe even thousands...) of holes. Relax, calm down – they won't suck the Earth (for now), because they are far away from us, but the very fact that they exist is strange. Two hundred years ago, practically no one would have even thought of such a thing as black holes, and if you went back in time and started explaining to people living in 1800 that the cosmos is as full of holes as your old man's socks, they would probably laugh at you.

Why? Because they were morons? No. It's just that the state of human knowledge at that moment was a bit poorer. So the existence of holes in space was unthinkable! Only a heretic (or any other theoretical physicist) could invent such a thing! But if something is "unthinkable", it means that it is impossible for a given person to think about it. Good, huh? I came up with it myself and it took me 26 years.

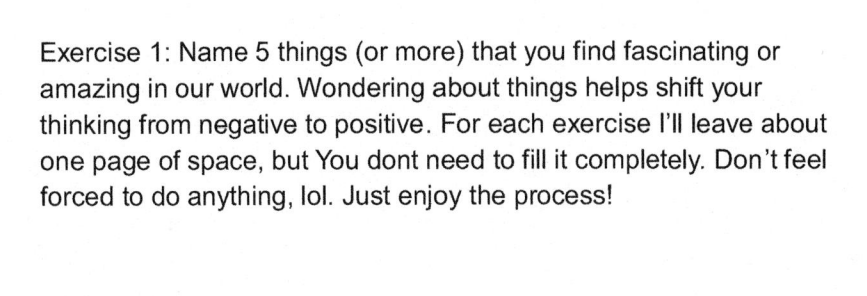

Exercise 1: Name 5 things (or more) that you find fascinating or amazing in our world. Wondering about things helps shift your thinking from negative to positive. For each exercise I'll leave about one page of space, but You dont need to fill it completely. Don't feel forced to do anything, lol. Just enjoy the process!

Nineteenth-century residents could not think of communicating with people living 2000 kilometers away using real-time video calls, and for us this is our daily bread. You can see for yourself how much technology and humanity in general have developed in a measly 200 years. What is 200 years? All in all, a lot, about 6-10 generations of people. That is, 6-10 new brains, each of which has better living conditions than the previous one, so they have more time to think about bullshit, and sometimes they come up with something useful. And sometimes it will make him schizophrenic, but a physicist is a risk, right?

To make you aware of the pace of development of this hairless monkey called man (sorry, Andrzej Dragan, I'm stealing this phrase from your book because I like it), I'll throw a curiosity (which I didn't take from Andrzej's book at all...)- Less than 70 years passed between the flight of the world's first airplane constructed by the Wright brothers (or other Left brothers) and the landing of a man on the moon – this is how quickly humanity develops thanks to knowledge. Yes, yes, I know – there was no moon landing, the Earth is flat, and pigeons are actually spy drones made by the government... But Elon Musk is planning to go to Mars in a few decades, maybe it's not a conspiracy, it's just the truth? Who knows? Or is Musk just a robot remotely controlled with 5G?

If someone didn't realize – it's just sarcasm. Humanity seems to have actually flown to the priest in an airtight mega corn can with a pointed tip, called a rocket, and pigeons are unfortunately not robots and shit.

And now think about it, how many people had to create such a rocket? Apart from engineers and a whole bunch of brainiacs, who sit in the office and drink coffee, and their delicate hands do not know the incredible advantages of hard, physical work (phi, amateurs...), rocket fitters had to build the rocket. By the way, holy shit – imagine being a rocket fitter, but it must be a fucking job... anyway – they had to assemble it from different parts, right? Someone had to produce these parts. Someone had to mine

AMELINIUM for these parts. Someone must have sharpened the tip of the racket, right? Someone produced the fuel for it, another engineer – the control system, and yet another – the system for throwing garbage into space. Such a racket is probably 10 times more complicated than a car, and I don't know about you – I wouldn't be able to assemble a car from scratch, it's so damn complicated. I couldn't even change the wheel (at the age of 19, so now I can), and when I was turning in the wrong direction, my friend tapped his head, tried the other one – and it worked. A miracle. See? That's why knowledge is important!

Exercise 2: List 5 things that are easy and obvious to you, but not to others. This will help you see how well you are doing in life.

It doesn't matter if it's a car, a bike or a toilet at the train station – every great thing is the result of the work of thousands (or maybe even hundreds...) of people. The company you work for also gives some "fruits" that are useful to other people. If your company actually produces fruit – then you give people bananas, tangerines and others... condiments. And if you work in a clothing company, you give the community shoes, jackets, pants. If you are a builder – your company gives people a priceless roof over their heads or a plant where they can work. EACH of us gives and contributes to this society, and society is constantly evolving. And the fact that, for example, people flew into space is not only due to the aforementioned brainiac with a big head and delicate hands (if anything, I have nothing against brainiacs, and I don't make fun of them, I even love them, but this book is supposed to be a bit sarcastic), who invented the rocket, but also all the farmers who produced food for the brain of this brainiac. Have you ever thought about it this way? Every single builder who has built any part of a house for any brainiac, or every mechanic who has built a bus or an airplane for a brainiac, has no less share in this success called the development of mankind than a scientist who has invented, improved, or created something. Think about how everything intertwines and how we all depend on each other. This makes every life meaningful and priceless – including yours. And it's even better when you have children – because, for example, your child can become such a brainiac and change something in the world. Then the success of the brainiac is in a way due to the mother, who bothered to give birth to him. Or maybe this success is also the fruit of the work of the brain's grandparents, great-grandparents of the brainiac, teachers, colleagues, or relatives of the brainiac? Who knows what's in the brain of a brainiac and what inspired them? Even if you recommend a book to a brainiac (about the brain, because the brainiac only reads them), YOU can be a part of his success, because without you he wouldn't read this book. God damn brainiac!

I have always been amused by typical older polish man, Janusz who watch a match of the Polish national football team (and you know , they suck, so what is he even expecting from them?), and when Poland loses, they say:

- Bastards, bastards! THEY lost! Again! Impossible!

But if they win:

- Yes! WE win! Maria, have you seen?! WE SMASHED GERMANY, FINALLY!

Got the difference? If they lost – Janusz say THEY did. If they won – we DID ;) But now I understand life a little better and I know that maybe Janusz is somewhat right in taking credit for the Polish national team, because the successes of some people are partly due to others. If you buy a Tesla, you are responsible for Elon Musk's success, because you gave him money for development. And same about Volkswagen, because you despise electric cars, you participate in the success of some lesser-known Germans.

- What? Me contributing in the success of the Germans?!- says typical, rasist, polish old man- Hell no, I'm selling my Passat! We buy a Skoda because the Czechs are our brothers! Germans invaded us long time ago, so they are not nice!

Of course I am kidding and I don't blame Germans for the things that their great great grandparents did, cause You should never blame a person like this. But, what's sad, many older polish people think like this and they have a victim mindset, blaming Germans for bad weather, lack of their life success, our polish alcoholism (like we would never drink alcohol, if not world war II, lol), and maybe even for their wife affair, who knows? Literally, victim mindset is so bad in them, that they have a great excuse for everything that fails in their lives. God damn, I stepped at dog's shit! THIS WAS A GERMAN DOG! Polish dog would never act like this! Holly molly, my boss fired me?! I think he is half german!

Anyway, at least, if we, poles, watch a footbal match with Germany, and somehow, by miracle, win, our euphoria has no limits! We like to think that someones else win is our win too.

And why am I writing about it at all? To encourage you to take credit for the successes of others? Well, no. But! NOTHING has ever motivated me or made me so happy in life as simply realizing that everything makes sense, we are all important, and we all create "something bigger". Does not matter if You are German or Polish or American- we all create OUR SOCIETY. HUMANITY! This is big!

The fact that we, or our children, have a comfortable life today is the result of the work of farmers, mechanics, builders or engineers who lived 50, 100, 200 or even 1000 years ago. And looking the other way – into the future – what kind of world our grandchildren or children will have is the result of the work of each of us. It is WE who create the world of the future. We can be proud of ourselves. Feel good about it – you are a wonderful part of something beautiful – humanity. It's true that humanity sometimes does some mania, but you would never do that, would you? So be proud of yourself and feel that life has meaning!

Exercise 3: List 5 or more things you give to this world. 5 situations where you helped someone, made them feel better, or did something good.

Chapter 1: The Pyramids, the Brain, and the Pyramid of Needs

What does the human brain consist of? Mainly fat. And that means I'm not overweight at all, just a big brain! Maybe I'm a brainiac myself?

And what does the human psyche and personality consist of? Of so many things that it's hard to list. When you want to take care of your brain, you eat a lot of olive oil and vegetables (both of these products have anti-inflammatory properties), but even if you drink olive oil by the liter, pour it into your ears and rub it on your eyes (don't do it, it stings), it won't automatically make you happy, brilliant, creative and full of energy. There is a little man in the brain called... You. And this man is a bit like a machine, because he is constantly programming him – in a better or worse way.

When as a child you listened to your parents constantly complaining that life is hard, the neighbor is a dick, and the president is a moron – it is quite possible that you will grow up to be such a malcontent yourself. But of course, this is not a foregone conclusion. You can stop complaining at any time, right? Why not? Something will happen when you smile at your colleagues in the morning today, instead of starting the day with the classic "Oh, if I only wanted to do it as much as I don't want to do it!". Maybe they'll you up because they'll see you as a smiling weirdo, but it's worth the risk. The smile is contagious.

Don't blame your parents if they actually "programmed" you the wrong way you wanted, because someone programmed them too. And since life was harder, looking back, the older generations probably had more problems and genuine reasons to complain than the younger ones. Today we live in golden times, and still few people appreciate it. When you go to the shower, you think it's the most ordinary activity in the world, but it's a luxury. Even kings could not afford a hot shower 300 years ago. When you buy products in the supermarket, you spin around it like shit in an ice hole, sad because you don't know what to eat today. Oh my, but you're poor, you have too much choice! Some people wonder if they will be able to eat anything, not what to choose. And hunger has been a very common problem over the years, millions of people have died from it. We are alive. As long as you live, it's allright.

Exercise 4: List the 5 greatest advantages of living in the 21st century. I know, life in our times has many disadvantages, but it is worth focusing on the advantages

People sometimes only look at the tip of their nose, so everything seems so important and personal to them. When someone tells you that you have big ears – don't despair. Maybe you really fucking have big ears? So what? There are people who don't have ears, so they would envy you. However, when you take every criticism personally and take offense at anything – think about whether there are really more important things in the world? Well, you're not the center of the world – and that's a bit comforting, don't you think? No one will die if you something up at work. Unless you're a surgeon, lol. Nothing will change if someone laughed at you today, insulted you, or reported you to your boss. Well, unless you get fired because of it because someone reported that you drank and stole (at the same time).

Exercise 5: List 5 unimportant, insignificant things that used to bother you but no longer bother you. This will help you understand that sometimes we overestimate the importance of our problems, and over time we learn to solve or accept them.

But in general, people today think about a lot of things, very intensively and often unnecessarily. Do you think that since I'm writing about it, I think I'm better and I don't do it? And in life. I'm a master of thinking, but about unnecessary things. I have a complex of two left hands, because my manual skills are tragic. To make it funnier – working on a construction site for many years, I didn't even realize that I wasn't very suitable for this job, because I wasn't very technical. I always thought that others were fucked up, because they quickly learn to use tools, they cut ventilation pipes straight, and mine look like pretzels, or how they hang these tubes – they do it in a straight line, and I create some eels. So every time something didn't work out for me at work, I thought and thought – WHY?! Damn! Why?! What can I do better? How to be better? How? How? How? Am I too lazy and not trying hard enough? Maybe I am not concentrating enough? Ha, from now on I'll drink 4 coffees a day, instead of two, to concentrate better. And what came out? It turned out even worse, because I was squirming like a vibrator. And every time I was sorry that someone was better than me. Because I was constantly comparing myself to people who simply have much more efficient hands. At one point, a friend told me:

- Damian, you have been working in ventilation for 4 years and you still cut the pipes so crookedly... What the hell is wrong with You?

And I said: Well, I don't know.

And it was a very good answer. If I wanted to learn something, but I didn't manage to do it for 4 years, I understood that maybe I would never know, that's just the way it is – and that's it. I don't have to be an ace in everything. I'm good at writing and I'm enough 😊 I would like to see how many pages of a book my colleagues would write in an hour? Come on, guys, let's sit down at our laptops and write! Are you better than me now, motherfuckers!?

Of course, this is a joke, because I don't want to compare myself to anyone and the whole point of this "parable of the boy who worked on a construction site, but had two left hands" is not to expect you to always be the best. From now on, when someone tells me that I cut crookedly, I say:

-I know. And I don't care. Fuck it. It will be covered by cealing anyway, so noone wil even see.

Kidding. I always correct fucked up cut with scissors, but I don't care if I am perfect, or not.

I reflected on my life and work and came to a simple conclusion – instead of feeling guilty about some pipes, I will just accept it. I don't mean that I will give up and from now on I will cut every pipe even more crooked, so that everyone can see what a master of neglecting work I am, but I just won't care about it as if it were the end of the world. Since no one has fired me from my job for it yet, it's probably not that bad. The tube can be improved. And besides, as real ventilation experts say: Nobody will shoot from it! And I love this approach.

But to justify myself that I'm not a lazy piece of shit at all, but I just think that the lack of aesthetics is also some kind of aesthetics, you need to know that a crooked cut of the pipe does NOT affect the tightness of the system at all, unless you cut it 10 cm too short, but that doesn't even happen to me.

Well, once I gave my friend 20 cm of pipe instead of 120 cm, but it was only because I couldn't hear what he was saying, I swear! In general, ventilation elements such as tees or elbows usually have a 3 to 5 cm "tolerance", because this is the length of the flange on which the pipe is inserted, and there is always sealing rubber at the end of the flange, so even if you cut the pipe two centimeters too short, it will still be tight. It will only look ugly. But in this case – you give a bottle of vodka to the Pole who makes ceilings, and you tell him to make this ceiling quickly in the place where you fucked up the job. After all, you come to work every day with a new bottle, because every day you fuck up your work in a new place. But who cares?

Exercise 6: Think of 5 ridiculous things that will happen if you screw up at work. For example, if you send the wrong order to a customer who instead of a double cheese burger gets a double lettuce burger, the customer will be 0.0001% healthier and will live 26 seconds longer, so in those 26 seconds before they die, they will still have time to tell their children that they are actually adopted! The dumber and funnier things you can come up with, the better. This will help you understand that sometimes our mistakes are just funny and it's no big deal if you screw up. So you don't have to worry about it. Write Your own funny stories here. The dumbest, the better! Allow Yourself to be riddiculus!

When I moved from construction to warehouse, I was one of the best employees there. And certainly the best one if the truck with bulk packages to unload was coming. Everyone hated unloading such trucks, and I applied for this type of work, because then I felt fast and hella strong, compared to my colleagues, and my ego swelled like rice flooded with water. Well, maybe every tome I agree to do hardest, unloading job, I allow myself to be used by my boss? Yeah! However, is it bad when both you benefit from something (because your ego is tickled) and the employer? No. This is the so-called win-win situation. The only person that loses is the truck driver, who could be on a long break if some freak didn't unload the goods in 3 hours instead of 5. Truck drivers threw tomatoes at me.

I really liked it (in the sense of work, not tomatoes), even though they paid so little that the ducks threw me bread when I passed by the pond, instead of me throwing bread to ducks – I loved this work.

I felt like a fish in water there, or even like a monkey in the jungle. When you plant a flower, a tree, or whatever, and that little motherfucker doesn't grow, are you angry with the flower? Well, no. You think to yourself – hmm, maybe it doesn't have enough sun? Maybe bad soil? So you don't blame the flower itself, but the PLACE where it was placed. You can think the same about yourself, because there are certainly places where you would flourish well. There are people with whom you would create a very, very happy relationship, there are jobs where they would appreciate you a lot. Don't blame yourself for your failures, because you're a flower. If someone blocks the sun from a flower or plants it on the wrong soil, it is no wonder that it does not want to bloom. On the other hand, don't use this thinking to shift the responsibility for all your failures and flaws onto the whole world, except for yourself, because you still have, after all, some level of control over your life. After all, YOU YOURSELF can choose your job. I'm assuming you're not a slave, are you? The flower is at the mercy of the one who plants it, but you are not. You still have free will. Probably. You can choose Your soil, get it?

When I started working as a dietician – oh, then I felt totally like a fish in water. You get it, people come to me, ask about something, I answer them, and they pay me. Awesome. I don't even have to lift a finger (unless they pay in cash, because then I have to move my hand to take the money). I use my knowledge, which I have accumulated over the years, and which someone will need to change their habits for the better. For example, when someone asks me how to lose weight (because of course they have tried everything), I say:

-Please eat less. And that's all. Now gimme my 1000 sek. Thank you.

-Holy shit, why didn't I come up with this myself! It's brilliant!

Of course, it doesn't look so easy (usually), and anything that seems simple (like eat less) is actually complicated. Because how can you eat less if your brain wants more? Oh, there are ways to do it, but this is not what this book is supposed to be about. On the other hand, it is often the case that things that seem hellishly difficult and complicated are actually simple. For example, sticking to a diet – many people find it difficult, because you have to count food to the gram and calories to the hundredth decimal place, right? Well, no. For example, you can follow the IF diet, where you eat whatever you want, but at the right time. And it works. Because you only eat 5 hours a day, for example, so no matter how much you want, you won't eat enough to gain weight. Unless you have a really big trigger. But even if you have it – over time your body gets used to hunger, regulates sugar levels and learns to burn fat, so you won't feel so hungry to eat who knows how much.

Okay, now give me my thousand swedish crowns.

Being a dietician is a really golden job, although it also has its drawbacks (for example, I am often irritated by people's laziness and the fact that when I give advice to someone and write out a diet, and they don't follow it, I feel as if my work is unnecessary...). You go into this kind of work with excitement, and when a patient describes their problem to me, I feel a bit like Dr. House, because I have to find some deeply hidden causes of his illnesses in his body, and then advise the patient on what to eat and what to avoid to make it better. Wonderful. I love it.

Exercise 7: List 5 things in which you feel strong, knowledgeable or skilled

If even such a lazy person like me could find a good job, I think that everyone will succeed, seriously. Some people, like me, have two left hands, so working with their hands will make them feel... Weak. So maybe it is worth working with the brain? Other people, for example, thinks that using brain hurts, but they are hellishly fit, fast and technical, so they will earn a lot assembling scaffolding or connecting electricity. Everyone has different predispositions and different needs, and this is again obvious. But I am writing about it anyway. And why write about obvious things? Let me explain! We live in the 21st century and we think about so much bullshit that we forget about the simplest and most obvious things. And it is worth reminding ourselves of this, as well as understanding it better. People are stuck for years in a job they hate, and yet you can literally change your job at any second. But typical, unhappy, sour polish man Joseph or Martin, who have been working for shitty polish work camp called "slavic-slave" for 10 years, which pays them the minimum wage, don't even think about whether they like this kind of work or not. So they live like this, mindlessly, like robots. And what can you do if you don't want to end up like this? Think. Just, god damn, think. I'm begging you to fucking think about it. Not about bullshit like crooked pipes (small details in life), but about the meaning of our life, what we like to do in it, and what we do. This is quite important, isn't it?

Now imagine that you are building a pyramid. You are a slave in ancient Egypt and you add another stone to a majestic building, when suddenly a colleague – Mohammed – tells you:

-You! Ahmed! This is crooked! Take it down, correct it!

-You yourself are crooked! – You reply

-Seriously, correct it, because our Pharaoh will cut off our heads if he sees what you've done here. Or maybe even worse – maybe we will get a warning from the boss!

-Don't be dramatic, mate. It's good. Get on with your work. Nobody will shoot from it!

And eighteen hundred years later, when the Egyptians repelled the onslaught of the invaders from Europe, they couldn't shoot them because someone had crookedly placed a stone on the pyramid. Then Mohammed laughed from beyond the grave at his colleague who botched the job.

But back to ancient Egypt, you work as Ahmed again. You have a coconut shell on your head (an ancient helmet) and a belt tied around your hips with tools made of dinosaur buttocks leather, because as you know, humans and dinosaurs walked the Earth together, right? It is impossible for the Flintstones to lie.

How do you feel when a colleague criticizes your hard work? It wasn't easy to carry that fucking 20-ton stone to the very top, let alone chisel it evenly with a primitive chisel (in fact, it took you a lifetime, because each slave had one stone to chisel), and this insolent boor says you put it crookedly. And what are you supposed to do now? To hit it with a chisel to even it out, for the next 20 years? A stone, not a friend. No way!

Exercise 8: Name 3 or more times when you thought you did something not well enough, but it turned out to be good!

Criticism of the work you do can hurt. If it's right, clench your teeth (or your sphincter, whatever is loose) and take it on your chest. If it is not right, and it only results from the fact that your friend is a malcontent, you have nothing to worry about. Here I am, a person who for years cared about criticism and cried into my pillow when someone saw that he had a pimple on his forehead (I'm kidding, I didn't do it at all!) I finally understood it, so I can confidently advise such an approach to others. The approach of accepting what you fucked up and fixing it, or the approach of ignoring what you absolutely can't change. As the wise quote says, "God, give me the strength to change what I can. Peace of mind, so that I accept what I can't. And wisdom – so that I can distinguish one from the other." A fat quote, huh?

Ahmed, whom you played for a while, is probably sad that for 20 years he hit a stone block with his primitive tool, and in the end it came out uneven. Cause 20 years of his life seems to be wasted now, right?

So think about how sad people must be who have been living for 40 years and think that something has not worked out in this life?

BOOOM. It's a very thick topic to think about, isn't it? Where does so much frustration in older people come from? Why are children very happy, even naïve, and older people are usually realistic, often sad? Because older people have a lot of expectations towards life, they compare themselves to others for years, and because of this, if they are worse in any matter – they think that something has not worked out for them. Or maybe it just turned out the way it was supposed to? Maybe you don't have to be a billionaire? You can, but you don't have to! If you're not, then well- that's how it turned out and that's it. If you had rich parents like Elon Musk, maybe the chance of becoming rich would be 50%, but since you were born into a poor family, that chance is only 10%? Maybe this life was just meant for you? Maybe hard physical work and years full of challenges were, unfortunately, intended for you, because someone had to do this work? You live in the 21st century, so you don't have the worst life anyway, believe me.

Ahmed (you) from the pyramids was screwed! Waking up at five in the morning, milking a goat to get milk (and goats stink), then drinking water from a dirty river (into which someone peed 2 meters away), and from six o'clock – working on hewing a stone. Hands swollen from holding the copper long, blisters burn and burst. You have to be careful not to get dirt into these wounds, because there was no tetanus vaccine or antibiotics at that time, so if you get an infection – you can even kick the calendar. If you want to wash your sweaty and dirty face, you wipe it with desert sand. There is no music that would make your time more pleasant. There is no TikTok to laugh at stupid videos during a break. The only thing you can laugh at is talking to your colleagues. A popular joke at the time was:

-A man asked a beautiful lady to sit on her lap and she farted!

 Haha. Tear of laugh. (seriously, there was such a joke somewhere, but I don't remember if it was written on Egyptian papyrus or in some book from medieval Europe). So evem jokes back then were poor. And you sit on Your stone on a break and get bored. And what do you do when you are bored? Think! About how hard this life is... eww, damn life!

Exercise 9: List 5 things you would do if you lived in ancient Egypt, but had the knowledge you have now, to improve the lives of people back then

Yeah, Ahmed. Enjoy Your boring break with no TikTok! Or maybe there is even no break? The pharaoh sees that you are in the back with your work, so he is the one who beats you in the back with a whip as punishment. And he tells you to work overtime, even though you are already cutting these stones 12 hours a day! The coconut shell falls off your head and as you get up from the ground after you've picked it up, you bang your head against your big stone until the horn (the perfect horn you've been cutting and grinding for 3 months!) crumbles and you have to do it all over again! Damn! You don't feel like it, so you leave it as it is. Then that scoundrel Mohammed comes along and criticizes your stone. You feel like picking up a 20-ton block with your bare hands and throwing it at your friend. You take deep breaths. You control yourself. You leave it as it is, just turn the chipped corner inwards so that it is not visible. Mohammed sees your manoeuvre and makes fun of you all the time:

- Haha, man, this is supposed to stand for 500 years! If you do such a mess, there won't even be 200 standing there!

You are boiling with anger.

But what did Mohammed and Ahmed not know? That the pyramid will stand for 4.5 thousand years, and people will still be delighted with it, although the stones have been eroded and none of them is perfect anymore. So no one even noticed that chipped horn. Ha.

Exercise 10: Name 5 things that are shitty, but people love them anyway!

Now imagine that your brain takes the form of a pyramid. I mean, not the brain, but the psyche. You see everything that is there accurately and clearly. You have access to it, you can add whatever blocks you want, or take some out. At the very bottom of your pyramid are the most important life needs, i.e. physiological ones that support the body, such as eating, drinking, pooping or sleeping. I don't recommend you to change this, because without these things we would die, so if food ever becomes too unimportant to you, because you will be so busy watching the grass grow that you will simply forget about food, then you probably won't be in for any good, comrade. And if you forget to have a bowel movement, you will burst. A shitty death. It is not without reason that our psyche considers the needs of the body as priorities, and when they are not there – we are slightly irritated or even anxious. The psyche serves the body (in fact, the body also serves the psyche, because the body carries the brain wherever it wants), so the brain will do anything to motivate you to eat or sleep, unless some mechanism in it fails. On the next levels, there are less important (but still important!) things that every person has to a greater or lesser extent – the need for security or belonging. You wouldn't feel good if you had an angry raccoon with a knife or a rat infected with rabies prowling your apartment, would you? Once you have food and sleep, your brain motivates you to get a safe place to live—so you work. However, there are people who have somehow let go of this level and are homeless. I'm not for me to judge whether it's their choice, a matter of laziness, depression, or just the malice of fate, but I'm guessing that no one feels completely safe sleeping on the streets, so I feel sorry for them.

Then there is the need for belonging, which each of us fulfills, taking care of ties with friends or family. However, if you have chosen the life of a loner (yes, you chose it because you prefer to be alone, and not because you hate people), you can organize into some groups, for example related to your interests, so that the need to belong is satisfied.

Then there is the need for recognition, and at the very top there is the need for self-realization. And this is where the stairs begin (although the pyramid probably doesn't have stairs...), because everyone can fulfill these two needs in their own way. Some buy fast cars and drive them like idiots, because they want to see recognition in the eyes of 15-year-old boys who are as excited about cars as they are by the sight of a naked woman, and others write books. Lol. I know it's a bit arrogant of me, but I dare think that writing a book gives a little more value than dangerous driving a car and buying one for show, but I don't judge, God forbid, reasonable people who have a passion for motoring and buy a car "for themselves", not for the audience. Then such a passion has more value, because the car is not only used to show off, but as a potential, good investment, or as a pleasant means of transport.

Some build themselves the house of their dreams, others travel the world, others record stupid videos for TikTok (and I don't judge that either, because I'm a fool myself and I like such videos sometimes, and I even recorded a few myself and then deleted them so that my friends wouldn't see). Some become surgeons to save lives, while others become veterinarians to save the lives of dogs, guinea pigs or cockroaches. Some eat tons of meat and work out at the gym to look like a Greek statue, while others smear tons of rejuvenating creams on themselves and go to the solarium to make their skin smooth as a glass ball. Some are vegan to save those animals that others eat, others

While during the construction of the pyramid no one paid attention to the microscopic shortcomings, because the Pharaoh was almost blind anyway and would not have noticed them (in fact, he wasn't), and a few millimeters this or that won't make a difference to anyone, because the pyramid is still standing (in fact, a few millimeters make a difference, and the pyramid is incredibly precisely built, that's why some people believe that it was built by some Martians or other

UFOs), so when it comes to the construction of your brain, even small things can count. What does a year consist of? From months. Months – from days. Days – from hours. And hours from seconds. If you think negatively for seconds, you will think like this for hours. Then for days. Months. And for years. That's why the little things matter, because as humans we are made up of seconds. And it doesn't mean that you have to walk around smiling every second of your life, but you know what it's all about – everything counts, because everything is part of a larger whole, just like every screw in a car is important, or every person in society.

Exercise 11: List ways you can easily help at least one person. In theory. You don't have to actually do it, but it can help you understand that you have many opportunities to make the world a better place, so your life matters.

If you cut off the top of the pyramid, it will still stand, because it will have a base, but if you destroy the base, the top will also collapse, because it won't levitate, will it? That's why people need to get the basics right first before they even start thinking about anything else. For this reason, not everyone in the Middle Ages had time to create inventions and explore the world in any way, because who would care when there is famine, disease or war, and first you have to ensure your survival at all?

For this reason, you may feel a bit of relief, because hardly anyone today has to fight for survival. Even if you have a very bad job and barely make ends meet, your life is not really in danger, because you can always steal something, get caught and go to prison where you will be provided with a hot meal. In the Middle Ages, they would cut off your hand for it and you would probably die of hunger, because no one cared about maintaining a freeloader then, and today even a freeloader has his survival assured – we live in such luxurious times! Of course, this does not mean that I encourage you to be freeloaders, but you know what it is about – it is really easy to survive. Unless you live in Europe and work as an underwater welder, you don't parachute off cliffs, drive your junk 200 an hour, and take heroin. Then it's half the battle. The basics are somehow guaranteed. We have the privilege and opportunity to develop and educate like never before, and yet only 7-9% of Poles read more than 10 books a year. Books are like the condensed life of another person, so it is not for nothing that it is said that whoever reads, lives twice. What's up! Three, even!

However, returning to the mental pyramid, it is worth realizing that our mind is not only made up of needs. You might as well form a pyramid of your beliefs. In the introduction, I already wrote why I think it does, but you can still disbelieve it and disagree with me – and there's nothing wrong with that. The meaning of life is a subjective concept and everyone can perceive it in their own way, or not feel it at all, but I would rather find it than not find it. Meaning is like gold.

Chapter 2: Gold in Your Backyard

Imagine that you live in the 17th century (there were no excavators back then) and drunk Uncle Cleopas tells you that you need to start digging a gigantic, five-meter hole in your garden – and right now. And it's winter. So you ask:
- But uncle! Why do you make me make a mad effort to dig such a pit? Is there any sense and purpose in this?
-It is, bruuuh! There are cat poop buried there!

-And why do we need cat poop?

-Well... You don't like cat poop?

-They stink like shit, so no! I mean- the smell of them is unpleasant for the nose!

In this situation, your motivation to get out of the warm house and dig a hole is about 0. But when Uncle Cleopas announces,
"Ha, I was joking! There is 10 kilos of gold buried there! We divide equally, so I take eight and you take two, and we are rich!
- But uncle! Where did gold come from in my garden?
"You may not have known it, but when I was young, I robbed a gold warehouse belonging to an Uzbek oligarch and then buried it on this parcell.

-Uncle, how did you know that I was going to buy this parcell? After all, I bought this property only 2 years ago!

- I didn't know. I risked.

In this situation, your motivation to mine is about 0.5 percentage points, because although the prospect of gold is tempting, you suspect that your uncle is just talking bullshit, so you still don't leave the house. However, when your uncle presents you with irrefutable proof that there is indeed gold in the garden (i.e. a letter that certifies that your uncle is wanted in Uzbekistan for stealing 10 kilograms of gold and smuggling it to Poland in his ass. Admittedly, the letter is written in a handwriting suspiciously similar to that of your uncle, but this is probably pure coincidence...), your motivation increases to 99% and you quickly rush to work, taking a shovel in your hands, breaking the ice sheet on the ground, and then digging. Because when you know that you have a reward ahead of you and your effort makes sense, you are able to endure even the greatest difficulties.

Such gold, only not buried in the garden, is the meaning of life and the good life in general. To want to work for it, you just have to be convinced that it is within your reach, and visualize such a life in your mind. But how do you find out if you're not convinced? Well, this is where skills help. You probably won't deny that someone who has high skills as a carpenter has a chance to earn more than someone who botches every job after that, like me in ventilation? Someone who has a course in dietetics, massage, physiotherapy or hairdressing has additional skills that will allow them to earn extra money, so such someone does not even have to convince themselves that they can have a better life. He knows it. A banker does not go to work convinced that he will be poor all his life, but rather focused on earning as much as possible, since he has the skills and the right job to do so. A lawyer is not complaining that he doesn't know what to do with his life and how to get money, but he is looking for ways to have more clients. The surgeon does not worry about whether he will have anything to put in the pot for his children tomorrow, he only operates, for which he receives a solid salary. As you grow and learn new skills, more opportunities arise. For an average Joe, becoming a surgeon is rather unlikely, but you don't have to go straight to 10 years of medical school, especially if you have no idea where the tibia and temporal bone are located. You can do quick and relatively easy courses covering your interests.

Did you know that light, moving from place A to B, "scans" all possible routes, and at the end chooses one? The number of paths that a beam of photons (particles of light) can travel is enormous, but for some reason the light "decides" to choose only one of them. This is not a theory, it is a fact. This is confirmed by quantum physics. We are also a bit like a light, because theoretically we have thousands of roads that our lives can take, but we are not able to live a thousand lives at once, so we have to decide on one of the paths. In the 21st century, there are so many opportunities to take up a job that the choice is huge, but it's probably better to have too many opportunities than none, or one, huh?

The problem is that most people may not even know what they want to do, why, why, how and when. People do not "scan" reality like light, but rather tend to be passive recipients of it. Meanwhile, in order to know which of the paths is the most profitable to take, it is worth scanning potential opportunities.

To know these possibilities at all, it is worth reading books again. Even watching movies gives you a new insight into reality, but books do it much better, because they go deeper into other people's experiences, thoughts and feelings. Reading them, you may have an epiphany and dream of being someone other than you are now, and then your motivation to develop increases. Then you see in your mind's eye the gold that life offers. If you don't see it, it's like you're blind, because it's out there somewhere, but you don't know where yet. Of course, life is not only about your own development. It's just as important to gain inner peace and maintain good relationships, so you don't have to be a pressure sufferer who feels like they HAVE to change things, do better, and do more, every day. You can develop slowly and with pleasure. Developing the mind through reading is probably the nicest form of combining business with pleasure. I don't know about you, but I like to KNOW things, and when I know how something works, I feel better.

Exercise 12: List 5 potential benefits and ways to a better life that are within your reach

There's a saying- If you have an hour to chop down a tree, spend the first 30 minutes sharpening your axe.

Personally, I would rather spend this time driving to the store to buy a chainsaw... But what if the store is closed? Then I would borrow it from a neighbor! And what if, for some reason, I have to do it with an axe?
Then the process of preparing for the action is as important as the cutting itself. And so it is in life. I read many biographical books with stories of successful people and I noticed that in fact, before they achieved success, they had been preparing for it for years. Charles Bukowski (an American writer and poet) struggled with alcoholism and depression for years, and published his first bestseller (the book "The Postman") only at the age of 49. Of course, for all these years he did not sit idle, but wrote (mainly things that he put in a drawer), honing his craft. The founder of Comarch (a Polish international giant in the IT industry), Janusz Filipiak, founded the company "only" at the age of 41, and became a millionaire at the age of 50. Previously, he was just an "ordinary" professor at the AGH University

of Science and Technology in Krakow. And I think he learned a lot, because knowledge helps to succeed.

It's not that you should expect a sudden, stunning success of yourself at the age of 40 or 50, because unfortunately not everyone can be famous and run a business worth millions like pretzels, but the important thing in life is that you can get better and smarter every day. You don't have to feel pressure in this direction and sleep 4 hours a day to read books for an additional 3 hours, because small steps after time give great results (snowball effect) and reading 15 minutes a day will also be okay, but it's important to have any goal at all and to pursue it in any way, even if you're dragging around like a drunken snail. A snail that consistently goes to its goal, day after day, for 10 years, will go further than a hare that sprints west for two days, then gets tired of it, lies down for three days, and finally decides that it is bored and runs the other way.

In the saying about the axe and cutting down a tree, you can see an allusion to life, because our mind is just like an axe. It is worth having a sharp and ready to act to make life easy. If your mind is cluttered with unnecessary bullshit, like whether to wear pink or blue or green or rainbow pants today, or watching other people's lives on TikTok, will there be room for the things that really matter? Think about it.

Stephen King, before publishing his first bestseller at the age of 26, wrote short stories for newspapers for years. Grandma Moses (an American artist) did not start painting until she was 76 years old, and her works found their way to museums around the world. One was sold for over a million dollars! Colonel Sanders (the founder of KFC) created the company known today only at the age of 62. Ray Kroc (the man responsible for the success of the McDonalds chain) discovered a small but very popular restaurant run by two brothers in their 50s. For years, he had various business ideas and failed spectacularly, but he never gave up. His wife was a little when he mortgaged the house to buy smoothie machines that offer the possibility of making up to 5 milkshakes at once, because hardly any restaurant had such a turnover that needed a machine with five nozzles, but Ray just thanks to the order for several such machines at once met the Mc Donalds brothers and went to deliver the machines to them personally, Because he was sure that they had made a mistake in the order and he did not believe that any restaurant had such traffic. Thanks to the creation of the MCD franchise chain and the fact that he managed the opening of subsequent restaurants of this chain, he became a millionaire. All these people were not born outstanding and rich, but worked hard for their success and each of them sharpened their axe for years. So if you think you have any chance of any success, don't worry about when it comes, just sharpen your axe day by day.

LEGO founder Ole Kirk Christiansen started out as a simple carpenter. For years, he built churches, houses and everyday products, such as ironing boards. What distinguished him from other carpenters, however, was the fact that he was an incurable optimist. When his house and workshop burned down, he did not break down, but built himself a new, better one. He didn't even have the money for it, but he had a trade in his hand and he knew that he would quickly pay off the loan on this house when he worked hard. When he was threatened with bankruptcy, he did not break down either. When the financial crisis came and he was living in poverty again, he still did not give up. He firmly believed that God would help him get through the crisis, and his faith gave him hope for better times. When his wife died of phlebitis at the age of 40, he struggled with a mental crisis for some time, which is natural, but he also did not abandon the company or his children, despite the fact that he had suicidal thoughts. When one day he saw that wooden toys were selling well, he got an order for several thousand yo-yos, he made almost all of them with his employees, whom he paid per piece, and then the company that ordered them went bankrupt, so they didn't pay him anything. And he didn't break down either. He converted all the yo-yos into toy car wheels and sold toy cars. Remember that this was the 20s of the twentieth century, so the production of yo-yos did not take place on a milling machine, as it is today, so each yo-yo was made by hand. Today, people don't have to carve wood with a knife to make them, so they are much cheaper and everyone can afford such a toy. At that time, however, both the wood and the carpenters' working time were valuable, and each unsold yo-yo was a small loss for the company, and it had thousands of them. This cheerful Danish entrepreneur sharpened his mind, perfecting his profession in hand, but also taking care of his four sons and running a business that initially employed 18 people. Then another fire broke out in his workshop, but at least some of the assortment was saved, and the house next door did not burn down. Ole did not give up again. When the war broke out, he joined the resistance and delivered weapons to the Danish partisans in LEGO boxes, even though there were two German occupying soldiers in his house who slept in a room with his mother-in-law. When a German officer came to take over his plant, Ole pretended not to understand anything, and... The officer left. Ole Kirk Christiansen raised his hard-working sons and gave them the LEGO company (this name, by the way, is an abbreviation of the words leg godt, meaning have fun in Danish), which was later inherited by his grandchildren.

Life offers obstacles, sure. But by focusing on them, you will fall into insanity, hopelessness, and depression. The mind in this case can be like your enemy. He tells you that life is hard, and you start to believe it. And in general, no one tells you to believe in something that harms you. Faith can always be changed, which is well known to Jehovah's witnesses. If they can convince people to believe in something that is completely different from the standard views of the average Janusz, maybe it is not so difficult to convince yourself to believe in something useful and nice? After all, you have more influence on your thoughts than someone who knocks on your door once a year...

If you don't believe it's actually possible to change the way you think, try self-hypnosis. I especially recommend the recording "Subconscious Programming According to Paul McKeen", which is available on YouTube. By putting yourself in a state of relaxation and listening to positive words, you will feel a big difference in your well-being after just 35 minutes, let alone after a month of listening to it every day? You see, if you can't "say to yourself" positive things and you don't believe in them (cool, it's not your fault, it's the fault of this fucking jelly called brain), then maybe you should at least listen to someone else saying positive things?

Exercise 13: List the 5 biggest difficulties in life that you have overcome. Try to remember how much strength it took. Feel proud!

This is not pseudoscience or wishful thinking, but psychology confirmed by research. In a study in which some participants filled out a questionnaire full of negative words, such as anger, sadness, depression, disappointment, failure, and others filled out a questionnaire filled with positive words, such as joy, pleasure, bliss, love, the mood indicators of the subjects were then measured with another survey, the positive ones actually showed greater levels of happiness. It's so simple that you don't want to believe it, huh? The brain is a primitive machine, ha. It may be a mega advanced mass of 86 billion neurons and an average of 1 QUADRILLION connections between them, but some things are simple about it, like the construction of a flail – you read positive things, you think more positively. You listen to nice books, you feel better. Someone gives you a compliment – and how do you feel? I'm guessing it's better than someone talking insults at you, right? So, allegorically, don't speak insults to yourself. Say (and think) nice things to yourself. I village.

Chapter 3: The Eternal Battle of GABA and Dopamine

Have You even seen the game of tug-of-war, but with cars? These are the "cars" you have in your brain right now. One of them is GABA – a calming neurotransmitter. The second – dopamine – one of the excitatory neurotransmitters. In each of us, they fight such a battle, almost constantly. One pulls the rope to the right, the other to the left.

And you know what's the weirdest thing about it? That while such a brain brawl can lead to depression (this is just a theory for now), most people believe that they have too little of both substances in their brains. Because if you have little motivation, strength to act and self-confidence, it's inevitably not enough dopamine, right? Pick it up, bull! yes, drink two coffees and burn three slugs! And if you have sleep problems and anxiety, it's not enough GABA! Raise your GABA by preferably drinking infusions of five different herbs – at least that's what a wise article on the internet claims, and the internet doesn't lie!

Of course, at the bottom of the article you will find sponsored links – one to a supplement with GABA (which I myself took for a long time, and swallowed them every day like my odlman swallowed pills for hypertension), and the other with a supplement with rhodiola rosea (which I also took), which increases dopamine. Are these supplements bad? Not at all! But does it make sense to swallow both if one of them stimulates and the other calms you down?

It is as if in one of the tug-of-war cars there was a Uncle Janusz, who presses the gas pedal to the floor, and when the car still fails, Janusz asks his wife – Aunt Marry – to eat some fries, and then, thanks to the force obtained in this way, push the car. On the other side, of course, there is a drugged Uncle Alfred and he doesn't give up, because he also pushes the gas all the way down, and when he sees that he is starting to lose, he breaks the windshield, throws the lasso on a tree and starts pulling himself and the car forward.

What happens to the rope between the cars? It is slowly bursting. What happens to the brains of people who drink eight coffees during the day, or take amphetamines, and at night have to smoke beer or sleeping pills to fall asleep? The same as with the rope. Did you know that the scientists who were the first to isolate cocaine from coca leaves took it and considered it a golden mean, a cure for fatigue, lack of mood and basically almost every other mental ailment? But then they realized that they were either getting sick or unable to sleep. Their drugged brains were already a little tired of this constant excess of dopamine. Some of them fell into other addictions, such as alcoholism (this time to turn off their brains instead of turning them on), and others somehow managed to quit the white powder, although it cost them a lot of suffering and often left permanent blemishes on their minds. But when they did, they felt like young gods. The problem is that such a moment of elation has its unpleasant consequences, because when the brain returns to the state of "normality", or even much below normal (because strained neurons die), they feel like shit with peas. And they are automatically motivated to reach for the next dose. Just don't laugh at them, because each of us does the same thing every day, only with different substances (I hope). Just don't put this book in your ass, because I'm not writing about it to blame you for it, let alone to suggest that you need to stop to feel happier. I'm writing this to illustrate how the brain works, and while it's better and healthier to live without cocaine, if you love it so much that you can't live without it—okay, I'm not judging. The same with sweets, ease.

When you eat sweets, dopamine levels rise, but after a while they drop again and you crave them again. When you smoke a cigarette, it won't be enough for you to be elated all day, oh no. After a few hours, you feel like "smoking" again, because just like with sweets and cocaine – cigarettes only temporarily raise dopamine. If a person addicted to alcohol drinks a beer tonight, tomorrow evening he will also want to drink a beer. Why? Because the brain likes MORE, HARDER, BETTER. Dopamine is particularly addictive because it is highly stimulating, but GABA (which is affected by alcohol and sleeping pills) is also highly addictive, because it strongly inhibits. Just think about the vicious circle in which my former colleague lived, addicted to both amphetamines and alcohol. During the day, he had a line to wake up, until at work he almost flew out of his pants, and before bed – two or three beers to make him sleep better. By the way – it's a myth that you sleep better after alcohol, because GABA breaks down quickly, and in addition, once used, GABA receptors are "blocked" for some time from being used again. The only thing alcohol gives you is falling asleep faster, which of course has its high cost.

But let's get back to the tug-of-war – why am I writing about it at all and why do I think it's a potential path to depression? Because we live in the 21st century, where we have (fortunately, but also unfortunately) a LOT of sources of easy and quick pleasure, and each of them more or less releases dopamine, which stimulates, and in order not to get the proverbial job from this stimulation, the brain tries to inhibit it somehow, i.e. compensate for dopamine by producing more GABA – which, however, works for a short time – so we have a lot of dopamine again, and little GABA. This makes us tend to live in a state of overstimulation.

That's why you can feel like shit even when you're unemployed and doing "nothing" for days, your brain is doing very, very, very (and once again very) a lot. It filters a lot of information, assimilates, remembers, forgets, associates, reacts, reasons... and so on and so forth. If I had to name one thing that inevitably and one hundred percent always helps me feel better, it is rest, but a real one – a walk without music, a deep sleep after a day without drinking coffee, an hour of bath during which I meditate, or anything else that engages the brain as little as possible. Even stupid washing of dishes or some monotonous work – during these activities the brain rests, as long as you don't think about twenty other things in the meantime. It's possible that we have an epidemic of ADHD and 80% of people can't focus on what they're doing, but maybe the world just presents us with so many challenges and opportunities that we always think about a hundred things at once and we're swamped with information like a toilet at the train station with corn from kebabs. Who knows? Maybe in the era of overloading the brain with thousands of short films a day, when feeling tired, instead of going to sleep, we bang our energol and smoke e-slug, and feeling sad, instead of allowing the brain to rest, we clutter it with even more information to escape from this sadness, the recipe for a relatively happy life is not MORE of everything, but LESS of what is not really important?

After all, when you stuff pebbles into a cup, there is not as much space for water as you would like. Water is YOU. This is what is important. The essence of you, consciousness. Pebbles are bullshit. The more bullshit, the less opportunity you have to focus on yourself.

When we are tired and want to work faster and more efficiently, instead of being stimulated by running or walking, we tend to hit an espresso (because it's faster), and when we want to calm down or reset, instead of naturally producing GABA with a nap or meditation, many people turn to alcohol because it replaces natural GABA. But the more GABA you have, the weaker the receptors of this substance, so you will return to a state of too high arousal anyway, but this time with less ability to calm down, since you have an increasing tolerance to GABA. So, holy shit, what are you supposed to do? Drink more and more? Some, of course, have chosen this path, but I don't think I need to explain why it's disastrous. At least not in Poland ;) A country where non-drinkers at a party look strange, and when you drink, i.e. flood your brain with toxin, it's git. I'm not a saint and I also like to pour my jelly-like lump called brain with a beer or two from time to time, but that's certainly not my lifestyle.

Exercise 14: Name 5 things that calm your mind and give you some happiness.

So if, contrary to popular belief, both too much inhibitory and brain-activating neurotransmitter can be harmful to humans, because paradoxically, the more, the weaker they will work over time, what could be the solution? Limitation of both. It is certainly hard, but doable. Not necessarily by strict fasting from stimulants (although you can use it) and avoiding any substance that affects the brain. It is possible that there is one, strange, brilliant in its action, quite well-known, although very underestimated substance, which reduces the synthesis of other substances in the brain! At first glance – that's bad, huh? Because what will happen if such a delinquent reduces dopamine, how will you work?! But still, this substance has been shown to have strong antidepressant potential, so maybe there's something to it? When you use it before bedtime, it works mainly at night, allowing your brain to rest from the constant struggle. In the morning, it will certainly be harder for you to wake up, because you will have less dopamine and adrenaline, but after some time you will get used to it, and you will sleep better. What is this substance? I'll tell you about it soon, but for now about something else, so that you can better understand how strange the human brain is.

I remember having a hard, stressful time in my life where I could hardly fall asleep, so I slept 2-3 hours a day for a week, and my brain was so devastated by this sleep deprivation that on the seventh day I could hear the voices of my boss and co-workers giving me orders, so I was afraid that I was starting to have schizophrenia. I decided to use mirtazapine (no, it's not this wonderful substance, the name of which I don't want to give yet), which is a very strong sleeping pill. I thought that since it was a sleeping pill, it worked on GABA, so it was very addictive. Fortunately not. Mirtazapine works by blocking serotonin and adrenaline receptors, so you fall asleep not because the brain is inhibited, but because it is NOT activated. Brilliant – I thought – and I decided that maybe if there was some natural substance that inhibits not serotonin and adrenaline, but for example dopamine and adrenaline, and even other neurotransmitters, but to a slight degree, so that you don't feel like a total, sleeping sloth like after mirtazapine for 12 hours, and you can use it every day, it would be nice. And there is such a substance! And I found out just today, of course, knowing this substance for years, but I would never have thought how wide its effect is. And God forbid! I don't think that this one substance is a universal, brilliant drug for depression. I'm far from being a "man of one substance" because I'm not naïve enough to believe that there is any single panacea for any disease. Most diseases are complex processes, just like our bodies. You can't say that, for example, cancer developed in someone because of consuming too much substance X and too little substance Y, because cancer is probably an accumulation of harmful factors A, B,

C, D, E... and so on, and the lack of a protective outflow of M, N, O factors... and so on. Similarly, depression does not have a single cause, and therefore no single drug.

- Did you eat too few vegetables?! Eat vegetables and thats all mate, your depression will disappear!

No. Well, it doesn't work like that. Although it can...

No, but no.

Now think of LSD, which dramatically increases the level of serotonin (the happiness hormone), after which (apparently, not that I ever used it...) people feel divine, but not from the pleasure and motivation itself, as after cocaine, but because everything is beautiful, poetic, interesting, deep and emotional. Apparently, it is impossible to fall asleep in such a state – and no wonder. The brain cannot sleep, both when it is overloaded with serotonin (happiness) and dopamine (pleasure), so it lowers them for itself before bedtime. Unless you bombard him every day with an excess of these substances...

And you know what makes things even more complicated? That dopamine and serotonin are competitive, i.e. they are opponents of each other. Too much dopamine (pleasure) interferes with the brain's ability to feel happy (serotonones). For this reason, instead of the eternal chase and taking part in the rat race, it is really worth taking a break from literally everything and a total, one-day detox from stimuli, during which you only sleep, read a book or walk in the woods. Believe me, it will do you a great job ;)

Exercise 15: List 5 things that you think are important to feel good about. Then rate how often you do them.

Chapter 4: A Brainless Life

You can also live without a brain. Or maybe even – sometimes it's worth forgetting that we have it? Just please, don't forget about it completely! Viruses, although they have no brains, are brilliant in their bizarre simplicity. Why? By attacking the host cell, the virus enters it and then forces it to produce thousands of copies of itself. Then the cell dies, and the viruses fly around to conquer other cells, like the local connoisseur of high-proof beverages who, after being kicked out of the bar because he was rocking in a chair and broke it, goes to conquer more bars. Fortunately, he doesn't have thousands of copies of himself and he doesn't (usually) smash the bar when he flies out of it. The virus, on the other hand, like a merciless torturer, destroys what it used to reproduce. Yes, it's brutal and ominous, so I'm not saying I'm a fan of viruses and I like to have the flu, but looking at it from a purely biological point of view, we have to admit that viruses are really clever. And now think about it – theoretically the worst shit there can be – viruses – because they mostly lead to human suffering and discomfort, and yet, despite everything, you can find something impressive and maybe even beautiful in them.

Their biological genius in simplicity. Viruses are the most primitive creatures on earth, even more so than humans, who enjoy harming other people. And yet, in their uncomplicated lives, they have achieved some significant success: they are the most numerous group of organisms on Earth. It is estimated that there are about 10 of them here to the power of 30, which is simply one and 30 zeros. There are about 10 billion viruses in just one liter of ocean water! If you are now thinking about giving up swimming in the ocean forever, let me reassure you that the vast majority of these ocean little crooks are bacteriophages, which means that they only attack bacteria, and are indifferent to humans. Or rather, they are beneficial, because by regulating the level of bacteria in the water, they purify it for us. So theoretically, you could purify undrinkable water with viruses and even treat antibiotic-resistant bacterial infections with them, which is quite ironic, don't you think? Usually, we associate viruses with something absolutely bad, and here we are – everything apparently has its purpose and serves a purpose.

But the funniest thing is that viruses don't even know they're alive. Firstly, because they don't have brains, which is obvious. Secondly – because it kind of... are dead. Scientists do not agree on whether they can be classified as living organisms because they do not have metabolism (viruses, not scientists), which means that they do not draw and process energy, do not reproduce themselves (as I mentioned, they need other people's cells to make proteins for them), they do not respond to stimuli and do not have a cellular structure. Exactly, a virus is not a cell. A virus is simply a genetic code (DNA or RNA) surrounded by a ball of protein. Strange, huh? It's like writing a message in a bottle, putting it in a ball and throwing it somewhere, let it fly into the world. And of course, he creates his copies, just to ... to make copies. For nothing else. The virus has no goal, or even a will to live, or the desire to succeed, nor does it seek happiness, nor is it afraid to die, nor will it be offended, as you call it an idiot. He doesn't care. It just flies around and copies itself. It's pretty beautiful if you leave out all the nasty diseases caused by viruses... After all, if you think about it for a moment – nature is incredibly complex, since there is something as funny and strange as viruses in it.

Exercise 16- Name 3 examples of things we could learn from nature and 3 at which humans are better than nature (for example- we use toilet paper).

And the people? They have slightly more complicated lives than the microscopic, infecting balls, but they also basically want to reproduce. And now a note, I'll give you an unusual perspective on life: I have a quite strange, but interesting philosophy that human life is not only about physically copying ourselves by having offspring, but also (maybe mainly?) about copying information. It's not literally about having to know as much as possible and copy every piece of knowledge into your brain from every book like an information junkie-nerd. Information does not equal knowledge, although knowledge is also a form of information. Everything around us is a kind of record of information, and the human brain is its recipient, transducer and creator of new information. Information is like clay – you take some of it and make pots out of it, i.e. your thoughts, experiences, emotions, and so on. Some may be crooked, others are rotten, others fall apart, but you are still sticky. Wow. Once in a while, something great comes out!

At the moment, your brain receives information in the form of letters, but apart from that – it understands it (hopefully ;)), because each of these words and sentences has its own meaning. Moreover, this meaning has to be interpreted by you somehow, so as you read, you create new sets of data in your head – new ways of understanding what someone else is writing. You are literally creating a new world full of new information. You, what you have in your head, is one big, new, unique world of sensations. It's beautiful, don't you think? It is wonderful that you ARE and have the chance to participate in it, having between your ears the most perfect, the most efficient and the most complex machine that man has ever seen – his own brain. If you've ever thought that your life is not worth much or something like that, ask yourself if you'd like to get a million dollars, but only if you die in a week? I don't really. And a hundred million and death in a month? I still don't.

What does that mean? That I value my life more than a hundred million. And why? Because I will probably generate much more value for the world during my lifetime. How much you value yourself is not that important at the moment (because maybe you just chose a million and death, and if so, don't worry – there is no chance that someone will give you such an offer in real life, don't order a coffin yet, mate!), because it's about the fact that the vast majority of people will not choose either a million or a hundred, only life. Why? Because life is so damn precious and beautiful that even when we are in its difficult moments, in a low, illness or breakdown – we still have literally millions of chances to change something and make it better. Literally every day, even when you're in the darkest ass and darkest depths of your mind, you can do anything good for the world, even the smallest thing – and that's priceless. Every day you can create new experiences – for yourself and others.

Exercise 17- List 5 of your most beautiful experiences.

The very fact that you experience something, i.e. experience something, is a form of copying data, because this data must get from the environment to your brain. And some can be copied indefinitely. Although a million people will watch the same film, the film does not decrease, just like the water from the river when a million people drink from it, because the film is pure information. And although there is only one film, there can be a million interpretations of it, because in addition to copying – we create new information, i.e. our unique set of data in the brain. Information is like viruses! They multiply and multiply! Especially when they share ;)

Everything we process is information. When you see a beautiful meadow, it's information. When you let off a momentous fart, that sound is information. When you eat potato pancakes – their taste is information. The virus is primitive, so the only data it copies is its own genetic code, from which little more can be said than that this code is a recipe for creating more strange balls like it. Why these BBs? And who needs it? And why? We don't know. There are just strange, small balls and that's it. Sometimes they kill something, maybe they cleanse the world a bit... Okay, all in all, they are somewhat necessary. Especially considering the changes in our DNA and the fact that without viruses we would never have been born ourselves, but more on that later. For now, for the sake of simplicity, we will assume that viruses are such small simpletons and scoundrels, because they have no brains (ha, losers!), and we, how great and wonderful people, have brains. Sometimes we even use them.

Fortunately, human life results in much more than the life of a brainless ball. Our lives are very varied and can be full of interesting events and contribute to the development of our species through our work.

Someone who has read a hundred books certainly has a more interesting life than someone whose peak ambition is to have a drink with friends on the weekend and watch football games, and the only book he has ever read is "100 Ways to Compensate for a Small Penis". Someone who not only reads a lot, but also travels, meets new people, plays new sports, and maybe even creates something himself, has probably "grinded" much more data than someone who only reads, so has an even richer life. Someone who works on a construction site and has contributed to hundreds of buildings has a more productive life than laissez-fairers who avoid work and want to do everything with as little effort as possible. On the other hand, someone who has a company and provides work for 10 people on a construction site, technically speaking, has contributed even more to the improvement of the economy than an individual worker, although of course both the efforts of the boss and the employee add up and complement each other.

Exercise 18 – list 5 things you would do as a company manager for your employees to make them feel better

People create systems, and the economy is one of them. It is a place where producers of goods and services (firms and their employees) and their consumers (customers) meet, and each of them derives some benefit from this exchange. Work is essentially a form of energy exchange, because you exchange your physical strength and your time for money. Shopping is also an exchange of energy, because this money is exchanged for services or goods. You have your goods, and the company has its money – everyone is happy. Theoretically, at least, because they could always push you bullshit...

Although capitalism, which is currently the most widespread of economic systems, undoubtedly has its drawbacks (for example, large differences in the well-being of life of the extremely rich and extremely poor), it also has one strong advantage – it inevitably leads to the development of humanity. People care about their own interests, so they work. Just think what it would be like if everyone got everything completely free – a house, food, entertainment... Who would want to work? Not many people. And how would humanity develop then? Slowly. Thanks to the built-in human desire to have the best possible life, we are constantly motivated to work, because it is what allows us to earn money and live comfortably.

What makes our lives much easier are inventions. And to invent something, what do you need? Apart from the brain, creativity and so on, of course... Information. Let's say that Elon Musk got the information that NASA basically completely ignored the topic of colonizing Mars and they have no plans to go there. Elon then remembered the information he had learned earlier that the Earth is sometimes hit by cataclysms. Then – he decided that it would be useful, damn, to have a plan B in the event of a serious cataclysm, such as escaping to Mars. And what would an average person do? He was worried that humanity would not go to Mars, and then he forgot about the matter and went to sleep, eat or watch TV. What did Musk do? He got angry. He was lucky because he was born into a rich family, which certainly gave him not only money to start, but also the right mindset – that in order to achieve something, it is worth knowing how to make money.

So Musk created PayPal, which is based on the exchange of information, because it is used to virtually transfer money in a moment. Today it is the norm, but it was not possible then, so PayPal achieved considerable success and Musk earned millions. All he did was make it easier for people to transfer information quickly, but that was enough and apparently of great value to people. For the same reason, Musk is a billionaire today, because he basically does things that accelerate people's development. Anything that speeds up our operations saves us invaluable time, so if you know a way to do something faster and more efficiently, who knows, maybe you'll become a billionaire too?

When he made millions from selling PayPal, he went to Russia and asked if he could buy old rockets from them. You know, it's like with a car – it doesn't matter if it shakes and rusts, as long as it drives. Maybe Musk made this assumption and wanted to go to Mars in a rusting tube with holes made of recycled corn cans? Who knows? Fortunately – proud Russian billionaires laughed at him and said that for these measly few hundred million he can only buy a villa with a swimming pool (phi) or jaht (phi), but not a rocket. Musk got angry again and decided to start building rockets himself. He read many books (he soaked up the data like a sponge, mayonnaise spilled on the floor) and what? The first few exploded, but who cares? Musk collected more and more information, until he finally learned how to build a rocket that not only does not explode, but also flies a little! And he is doing better and better. In the meantime, he bought and developed Tesla and worked on the Neuralink program. The latter company implanted a chip not so long ago into the brain of a paralyzed man that allows him to control the computer cursor with his thoughts, so now this man certainly has a much easier way to exchange information with the environment. It's inspiring, but I'm not writing about making you feel inferior to Elon Musk and have some unhealthy, excessive pressure to succeed. On the contrary – there are people who have some talents (and rich old ones...) so they achieve above-average things, and... There are their customers – ordinary people, as important as the creator of the business himself, because without them the business would not be going. We all have a place in the system, and if you think your place is at the top of the pyramid, like Elona, go ahead and show them! You are a winner! Or maybe you have too big an ego, who knows? No, what am I talking about, you wouldn't let your ego take over your life in your life, right?

However, if you are humble enough to admit that your place is at the base of the social pyramid (like 90% of people), remember that the base is the most important in the pyramid and it is the one that lifts the top, not the other way around. It is the builders who build the houses we sleep in, the farmers who produce the food we eat, and the factory workers who make the cars we drive. The people at the base of the pyramid are the most important. Elon only gives amenities and innovations that are great, but without which you could live. And without food or housing, not entirely, so this – in a way, a builder gives the world more than Musk. Phew, a billionaire of some sort... I could do it too! No, well, joke. Either way, no matter where you stand in the pyramid, be proud. Understand that life is not just some strange, meaningless story – life has meaning, and you are part of something great and wonderful, while your contribution (whether it is goods produced, services rendered or children born) to society will be forever recorded in the pages of history. Each of us interacts with the world every day, which drives its development a bit. Nowadays we have so many comforts and entertainment, because 50 years ago, 100 years ago or 200 years ago our ancestors... they just lived. And when they lived, they worked (because they had to), and when they worked, they developed the world. That's why we have such a nice time today. Many people fall into the trap of thinking they're slaves when they're not, and work is yuck! No, it is not. It's unhealthy to think like that, and you'll get a job from him, seriously. Your job is there to make it better for someone in 100 years, and you have the right (and even the duty!) to feel proud of it, regardless of whether you are a professional broker, the king of toilet seats, or perhaps a world-famous analyst of cricket chirping.

Humanity in the 21st century has millions of opportunities to spend time in a pleasant or useful way, and what once seemed to be an element of an SF movie (for example, video calls at any distance in real time) is now considered the norm. As the economy grows, more and more inventions make it easier for us to send our thoughts and words to others. In the past, you would have to use a pigeon to send a friend from across the seven seas birthday wishes. The pigeon, as you know, may not be fully aware of which person is your friend, so you would not be guaranteed success with such a shipment. Later, when the time of the "postman" profession came, you could send wishes by post, but they also took quite a long time. And the postman could be drunk and mistook the address... Today – a few clicks and wishes fly to the other end of the planet in a second. Just think how great an achievement this is of our civilization! And why was such an achievement possible? Because people worked! They created more and more of all sorts of metal shit, buildings, cars, computers, and so on, until eventually the possibilities of construction, engineering, information transmission, and programming became so great that they could create a creature called the Internet, requiring hundreds of kilometers of cables (or maybe even dozens?), thousands of computers, some code, and a hundred heads to do it. Oh, and thousands of volts of energy that someone has to produce and transmit somehow, and the cooperation of thousands of people who create websites, and of course millions of people who use it and make it profitable. Yes, that's us.

The Internet is, of course, a key innovation that serves many purposes, but everything that has great advantages can also have its drawbacks. In this case, the downside is the excess of information, from which you have to filter out the true, effective and necessary information. For example, if you want to learn how to make an apple pie, you'll probably come across hundreds of recipes, but Google will do half the work for you, filtering out unpopular sites from well-known ones, so you'll find a good recipe almost immediately. But looking for a recipe for happiness... you may be a little disappointed. There is no single, unique recipe for every feeling, there is no magic pill or device that will reprogram your brain and make it notoriously happy. The brain itself can work against you, producing too little happiness hormones for some reason, and although there are drugs that increase their level, they do not work forever, on everyone, nor are they a solution to problems, but only a temporary solution. For this reason, we have to discover the recipe for our own happiness ourselves, and this is a damn difficult (although also instructive and developing) path.

We look for things in life that are exciting, interesting, informative, inspiring... and this is where applications like TT, Facebook or Instagram come into play, which give us the opportunity to absorb thousands of different pieces of information during the day by watching short fragments of other people's lives, even through short video materials. Wonderful, right? Everyone is looking for something different in them, because everyone has different niches of interest, but one thing is unchangeable – we want to enjoy it or gain useful information. And how many of these short videos will really be useful to you in your life, since most of them are satires, funny cats, someone's mishaps and falls, or people bragging about their biceps, cars, or how much cake they can eat in an hour? Take useful information from it here... Maybe this flood of unnecessary content is not so miraculous? Maybe it fills our brains like a computer's memory, which an unreasonable user has filled up, downloading a ton of viruses to the disk?

We are currently too overloaded with stimuli and there is no doubt about it. We use our brain every day, intensively, non-stop. Somewhere in all of this, observing the outside world, thinking about it and taking part in the greatest waste of information that has ever taken place in the history of mankind, we forget about the most important thing – ourselves. There is so much different, interesting crap in this world that it's hard to tear yourself away from it and find at least half an hour for... sitting in silence. When was the last time you really did NOTHING?

Imagine that consciousness is water in the ocean. Your body is like a cup into which this water is poured and takes its form. An empty cup can hold, let's say, 250 ml of water. And what happens when you stuff pebbles, gravel, sand and so on into a cup? There is not so much space for water there. Life in the 21st century is full of such pebbles – things that we want, that we think about, that we focus on. The more of it all in us, the less room we have to be aware of ourselves.

And of course, I'm not a fan of extremes and I'm not saying that you have to get rid of material things and all your dreams or expectations, and then go to the Bieszczady Mountains and live like a monk, beating the gong eight times a day and meditating until you start flying. No. But think about whether we sometimes go to the opposite extreme – clogging the mind with so many things that there is no longer a "us" in it. And when you take a break from it for a moment, you take deep breaths and say:

- I am.

And then you will feel it – this affirmation can make you realize a lot, although it is trivially simple. But what is it that makes you realize?

That you exist! And that this is what power is.

Viruses are dead, they are not aware of their existence, so they do not think about it, and yet they exist. And they reproduce on an unimaginable scale.

So maybe human life, full of thinking, analyzing, evaluating, conjecture, theory, plans and dreams, would become more effective if it simply relied on life, not on thinking about life? On feeling that you exist, and not on forgetting about it because you focus too much on the outside world?

Exercise 19 – List 5 affirmations that you believe in and that you can repeat to yourself

Chapter 5: The Two Sides

Imagine that you are writing a book. Your readers, of course, don't want to read shit that will somehow bring them down, make them depressed, make them lose the meaning of life... and so on.

So your mission is to make people feel good about reading these excerpts of yours. You want to make them laugh, because laughter is health. But nowadays we have so many funny videos on the Internet that we laugh at literally every stupidity.

- Haha, someone put a banana peel on the ground and someone stepped on it and slipped. Haha, I can't help laughing!

- That's nothing! I saw how the peasant dressed up as a woman! Haha!

-This... it's nothing! I saw a video of someone giving a monkey a candy, and when she reaches out for it, the man takes it away at the last moment and the monkey gets angry, haha!

Cool, cool. We laughed, laughter is health. Maybe you can actually cure depression by watching funny comedies twice a day? I doubt it, but you can try, because it probably won't hurt.

But you probably won't make anyone a better person just by making them laugh. Laughter is just a moment – you laugh, it's nice – and you forget.

So you would like to give your readers something that will stay with them for a long time – knowledge, inspiration, motivation... and so on.

And now imagine that this hypothetical book you are writing... it's your life. This book is your brain. What do you write in it? What do you give yourself? Is there any inspiration, any deeper purpose, or any desire to strive for something? Or maybe you delude yourself that life will be good if you only laugh at least 20 times a day, binge-watching short videos on the Internet... and nothing else? Maybe sadness and lack of purpose in life come from the fact that we don't even look for purpose or happiness, because we are busy with nonsense bullshit, writing down our book called the brain with a thousand words we don't need? So, although short videos on TT are funny and cool, it's also worth seeing the other side of the coin – they can distract you from what's more important, and take up your time. Many of them are also soaked in negativity, so they can be harmful to the psyche. What you surround yourself with, you become. So I doubt you will become happier by watching morons every day and squeezing them in the comments that they are morons. However, if you watched outstandingly smart people and congratulated them in the comments, you would have the right to feel the s8 better after a while, because apparently the brain does not distinguish on a subconscious level what you say to others from what you say to yourself. So if you tend to criticize everyone, consider whether you're doing more harm to yourself by being your own enemy. I mean, it's your brain, not you, of course you wouldn't do that in your life, right? And the brain is just an information grinder, and when it sees negatives, it tends to react negatively to them. This can be mastered simply by not exposing oneself to negativity, just as a person on a diet can control their cravings for sweets by avoiding the smell and sight of them. Life may be hard at times, but don't forget about the other side of the coin – it can always be easier. When you work at Januszex, which not only generates a lot of stress in you and pays you pennies, but is also full of negative people (I have worked in such places and I know what it's like), you have a choice of two approaches – either I grit my teeth and force myself to go to this job every day, or I find a more pleasant one. That's what. There are always at least two possibilities and two perspectives to consider, and only a fool closes his mind, limiting himself to one.

I like to see two sides of the coin in everything, because then I have a comparison and a better picture of the whole. The first example of a situation where it is really worth noticing these two sides is work. You spend a large part of your life in it, so naturally – it's better if it is beneficial for your brain in some way and does not "write" negativity in it, but rather positivity.

To be honest, I was extremely unlucky when it came to my first jobs. I abandoned, for quite complicated reasons, my plans to study pharmacy in Poland, went to Sweden and started working on a construction site. Not having much choice and not knowing Swedish, and speaking English at the beginning at the level of a moderately smart monkey, I took the first job that was offered to me.

And of course, it was full of negative people. Soaked with venom to the bone. Soaked in regret for life, regret for ourselves. Enslaved by addictions, torn apart by anger, like the boxers of drunken Uncle Staszek, which tear when the stitches are stretched to the limit under the pressure of his buttocks, when Uncle Staszek crouches down to replace the pipe under the sink.

Of course, I can't generalize, because I also met some good, intelligent colleagues on construction sites. But unfortunately – they were rare.

Every day on my way to work, I felt strong stress and anxiety that I would get a task that I would not be able to do, so they would look at me askance again. Either that I would do something stupid, or that I would not understand something, or that I would break something. Or, in the worst case – that I will be in such a hurry and overwhelmed by stress that I will fall off the ladder and break my neck. I was also irritated by my friends constantly complaining about everything, and if you get among the crows, you have to crow like them (or them), so I started complaining too.

When I entered the construction site, I usually heard:

- But I don't feel like it!

- We're doing this shit again!

- Why do I have to do this? The boss is a dick!

- But these tools are overridden! Why didn't this moron buy us better ones?!

- He pays me so little, and expects me to do the job so quickly?! Well, moron. Well, a pitcher. Idiot! If I had a company...

- I don't give a! I won't listen to this moron!

- Youngster, you are not for thinking, you are for work! We'll do it my way! Yes, it will be harder and maybe a little more dangerous, but faster!

- Hurry young! I want to finish it by 3:00 p.m. and leave an hour earlier! What are you doing so slowly? Fuck!

- Learn yourself, I don't get paid to teach! When I started, I had a week to study, and after a month you are still learning?!

- Oh young, young... Your generation can't do anything!

- Oh young man, THINK A LITTLE! (And I'm not for thinking)

- How do you hold this hammer!?

- Fucking hell, the electrician stole our ladder! What a moron! Kid, go tell him in English that he's a moron and that he should give back the ladder or I'll fuck him up!

So I went and said:

- He says that You are awesome, but we need our ladder now, can You give it back to us?

- Yeah bro, no problem!

-"And? Huh, young man, did you tell him?"- asked my fucked up polish mate

- Yep.

- Is he scared of me?! Will he give it back?

- Yes, as soon as he'll change his pants full of shit, because he shat himself out of this fear, U know?

Exercise 20 – List the 5 stupidest reasons to complain that you have heard

In addition to such typical moments of complaining about work (in which for some reason these people were stuck for 12 years and didn't change it, lol), there was also a lot of complaining about the fact that this colleague is an informer, that one is a dick, and the third one doesn't know anything. Sad confessions about his private life, that someone's wife is rude to someone, so he cheats on her, or that she didn't cook him dinner yesterday, and according to him, it's HER DUTY. Philosophical thoughts over a cigarette about the fact that life is bad, hard and brutal, and only the toughest survive. Attempts to influence me and convince me that I need to rebel more against the system, my boss or even my own girlfriend, because everyone is bad and wants to me. Oh, there was a lot of it. I've listened to all kinds of shit and believe me – I had many reasons to fall into deep grief and sadness. Sometimes I would drop by. yes, it's natural. Yes, it's normal, everyone has the right to do so. You can't blame yourself for your bad emotions, no no no. But you can also learn not to be stuck in them and delude yourself that life will change for the better when you sit on your ass and don't change anything.

I really deeply regret that I did not keep a notebook at that time, in which I would write down all the texts of my colleagues and all the strange problems that we encountered on various construction sites. This would result in at least 3 thick books analyzing the causes and effects of human negativity. Comedy-drama. A grotesque parody of construction work among people who can't work sober. One has to hit a beer in the morning, another has to punch his nose. And yet another – he despises these alcoholics, but earns extra money on the side, selling them beer illegally imported from Polish. There was such a delinquent.

But then, after five years, I found a job that seemed perfect at first. Not because it was easy or less mentally taxing. Because the atmosphere in it was incomparably better. Not perfect, but still - enormously better.

People were just smiling. Instead of saying that they didn't want to, or that our warehouse was a pile of shit, they tried to stay positive. Everyone thanked everyone for their help, everyone wanted to teach me something and help me when I started. Everyone insisted that I ask for help and ask when I didn't know something.

Then I also saw the other side of the coin – how much influence the people I surround myself with have on my well-being. Because while working on the construction site, I still told myself that it was not so bad. That I will NOT let negative people affect my mood. But I still gave.

And working in my new job, in a warehouse, I was happy to let the positivity and smile of others put me in a good mood. I think I was one of the most negative people, because when I failed at something or felt that I was doing something too slowly and ineptly, I got irritated. But no one blamed me, no one criticized me, no one put pressure on me.

For a few weeks, I went to this job with excitement, mainly by newly-met, intelligent people who always had something interesting, wise and funny to say, always had a positive effect on me and made me gain new, valuable perspectives on life every day. I think that if these people somehow read this book, they know that it is about them.

For several months, new, valuable information appeared in my brain. I coded and wrote down a completely new truth, shocking to me – work can be enjoyable. Work can be nice, and people are not angry, bitter and mean. People can really be nice. Wow.

Even people who have a lot of problems themselves. They struggle with the demons of their own psyche, but despite everything, they are able to maintain a positive attitude towards their co-workers. It was so incomprehensible to me!

When I was going through a big mental crisis, I pretended that everything was fine and also tried to smile and be positive to my co-workers so as not to infect them with negativity, but a few people noticed that I was down. They asked me how I felt, if I needed anything. They asked why, what happened. They wanted to help. They said I don't have to hide my emotions, I can be angry and negative if I feel that way. They said they understood me. That I have the right to be angry. That it's human.

Hearing this, I almost cried, because I believed again that there is good in many people. It was impressive, especially considering that those people who were the nicest had the most problems themselves, and I was never able to help or advise them in any way, and I was even afraid to ask about too private matters so as not to look nosy.

So I've met good people and I'm damn grateful for that. If I knew the detailed history of each of them, I would write a book about them, because they deserve it. They are outstanding, each in their own way.

So what has changed from my personal life book?

My perception of work, people, society and life in general has changed. I realized that I could never again allow myself to have something written in my mental book that destroys me, makes me depressed and hopeless, or fills me with hatred for the world. I understood that I had to make every effort to surround myself with good people and cut off negative people mercilessly.

And why am I writing about it? It's simple to warn many of you. Hard, physical, stressful work is not always bad. All you have to do is do it surrounded by positive people. And not always a light, well-paid job is good – if you are surrounded by people who pull you down in some way.

Don't let someone else write some shit in your personal book! Don't make that common mistake that I and many people have made.

Other people's mistakes are there to learn from them and not to have to make them personally.

I don't like to think that any years of my life are wasted, because for sure every day is a lesson, but looking at my life critically, I have to admit that yes – I wasted these five years a bit. I wasted it dealing with negativity and absorbing it like a sponge. And I wasted a lot of my health smoking cigarettes and drinking alcohol with people I should never have drunk with.

But as they say – there is nothing bad that does not turn out for good! At least that's what I tell myself. Gradually, I feel that I am getting back on track. Mainly by changing the perspective on people, but also by focusing more attention on inner peace, learning and understanding many new things, and above all – by choosing a new goal and believing in it. Sometimes, development, paradoxically, is about doing nothing, just giving yourself time to rest. If "depressed" sounds like DIP REST (DEEP REST), maybe that's what a depressed mind needs? Maybe depression happens to those who have already burned out, so it's a defense mechanism that forces you to rest? So if you are depressed, or wondering if you have it (i.e. the situation is not very interesting anymore), give yourself time to rest. I write about development and change all the time, but you need to know that I don't expect you (so don't put such pressure on yourself either) that you will do more and more, even if you don't have the strength. Maybe do less, but do what is nice, important and beneficial, instead of what burdens the brain and generates stress? Instead of watching short videos for 2 hours, which clutters your mind with shit, you can go for a walk in the woods for an hour, which refreshes and soothes your mind, and thanks to this you have another hour to rest and do nothing. Maybe the purpose of life does not have to be a sprint and a run for everything, but a leisurely walk? Maybe positivity is achieved not through sudden, stressful life changes that require a lot of willpower, but through small, easy steps? After all, easy and slow steps work, precisely because they are easy. A super difficult cabbage diet is difficult to maintain for more than 2 weeks, because it requires hellish willpower, but for example, the IF diet, which does not require counting calories, can be maintained for months. By the way, such a diet potentially heals the mind, because it increases the production of BDNF 1 (a hormone that builds new neural connections).

Maybe before you become happier, more positive and energized, you have to pretend for a moment that you are really like that in order to switch your brain from looking for flaws in people to looking for their virtues? To be honest, I hated people for many years, but gradually I learned to accept and understand them, and maybe even love them a little. And if you love others, you also love yourself. I didn't do it suddenly and overnight, but slowly like a snail, looking for good in them instead of evil. Instead of bombarding my brain with shorts and other short videos, where every second comment is criticism, and also commenting myself, criticizing criticism, I uninstalled apps with videos in my cunt, and I admit that it's very beneficial for the brain. I read books instead, I don't get bored!

My goal is to be a positive person. So that I can change people for the better with this positivity. Trivial? So think about it, how many positive people do you really know? They are rare. It's hard to be such a person in today's world, but it can be done and it's worth it. Sometimes it is worth applying the principle "Fake it till You make it".

Because when you are negative, people will be negative too. And when they are negative – you will become even more negative. And when you become like that – so do they. And this is, my dear, a harmful vicious circle. You can't run away from it until you stop it. It's YOU who has to take the initiative and start thinking positively if you don't want life to be negative.

Exercise 21- List your 5 simple goals. If you don't have any – think of something absurd, like „I will do 30 jumping jacks today". Every, even the stupidest, accomplished goal increases your satisfaction with life, sense of control and motivation to do something more. The brain loves the feeling that it is achieving something.

Chapter 6: Something and Nothing

What do you think is currently one of the most effective, longest-acting and at the same time fastest-acting medications for depression? Maybe it's SSRIs (selective serotonin reuptake inhibitors), i.e. drugs that increase the levels of this important happiness hormone in the brain? Unfortunately – no. As I mentioned earlier, they don't always work. And they need about two weeks to start working. They won't change your life or your thinking, because if you hate your job, people or the world, you won't suddenly start loving them. You can get a temporary kick of the will to live when you take SSRIs (and God forbid I'm not against using them when necessary, because it's better than deep, destructive depression), but still, you have to get out of the swamp you're in. Psychotherapy and regular contact with a psychologist are hellishly important in depression, and even for people who don't have it, but just want to feel better and be heard. Never give up on help when you can get it. However, when your psychologist (for the National Health Fund) tells you: it's nothing! I'm having it worse! – maybe it's not perfect and maybe you can change it for the better? In the same way, not every SSRI drug works for everyone, so if a drug causes a lot of side effects and doesn't work very well, ask your doctor to change it, that's what.

As a curiosity (because maybe such a therapy is not recommended for everyone, you have to consult it with a doctor if you want to try it) I will write that IN MY OPINION THE MOST EFFECTIVE, BUT VERY CONTROVERSIAL AND IN MANY COUNTRIES ILLEGAL DRUG, which after just one use pulled many patients out of deep depression, is a mysterious substance, after taking which the feeling of one's own body disappears, because nerve conduction is partially inhibited by it, so it does not increase your level of happiness, but allows you to feel for a few hours as if you do not have a body, because you do not feel it. Your "I" also partially disappears, and with high doses you even stop remembering who you are, where you are and what the world looks like in general. So how does such a strange experience treat depression?

It seems that after taking this substance we should feel less and less, and yet the opposite happens. People who have been lucky enough to try it describe it as if they suddenly feel like they are a vast field of energy, a spill of water, or a great cloud, and not a body. I imagine it like being water poured out of a cup that pours into the ocean. Then, when the feeling of the body gradually disappears stronger and stronger, and the psyche "dissolves" into nothingness, patients using this drug describe a state called "k-hole", i.e. being in the middle of an endless, complete, infinite emptiness, and being this emptiness. Being empty! Do you understand any of this? Because I don't! And it is not a terrible, dark void. Not at all. People describe it as the most soothing, peaceful, and beautiful place imaginable. They feel "at home" there and experience absolute ecstasy. Maybe this is what is so soothing and healing? Just the awareness that such a thing exists? It must be very interesting. But why am I mentioning this?

I was talking about this substance with a friend of mine, who by the way inspired me to write this book (thanks, Danny!) and I just talked about what I recently heard while watching YouTube – the state of the k-hole. I described it as strange, because, since you are "emptiness" and there is nothing around you, and you yourself are also "nothing", it should not be possible to experience or remember this state, because in order to remember and experience something, you must have a mind, and when you are not there, there is no mind, so no experience! So I was sure it was a kind of paradox.

Danny just said,

- And what do you think consciousness is?

-I do not know. Nobody knows! Something...

- Or maybe nothing? –He asked

- How can it be nothing?! Haha! -I replied, thinking he was joking.

- Think of it this way- The finger cannot touch itself, and the eye cannot see itself. So maybe in order to experience "something" we are really nothing? Because if we were something and experienced something, it would be as if your finger was stroking itself. Understand? Maybe "nothing" is a pure source of our consciousness and we come from this emptiness they describe? From nothingness? WE are the void, and expiriencing something is possible, cause it's outside of us- nothing.

Then I was struck by the weight of these words and I had a little epiphany. If you've read my previous book, you know that I was analyzing a philosophical problem there—how could something come from nothing? (Our universe) and I came to the conclusion that it could, but only on the condition that something and nothing are not two completely separate, different states, but simply different intensities of the same state – just as heat and cold are not completely different things, but only a certain intensity of temperature.

So what if we mistakenly ask – what is after death – "Something or nothing?", when there can be both? Maybe one results from the other, one is intertwined with the other?

Yes, it's quite logical – I decided and finished my thoughts. But I never thought that "something" could be the outside world and we could be nothing. Because that would be weird, huh? How can I be nothing, if I feel like something! Well, maybe I feel like something cause I am just constantly expriencing something in my mind, and pure being is actually being nothing. Weird?

Well, not exactly. Buddhist monks came up with this idea a long time ago, but when they describe it in their books, it's very, very difficult for someone who hasn't experienced it to understand. How can being in nothingness be better than being in something?! - you will think.

People imagine "nothing" as a cold, scary, black place. As an abyss. But thing about it- how can we assume that nothing is scarry? Well, maybe nothing is the complete opposite of our imagination?

When "nothing" limits you – what can you do? Everything!

When "nothing" bothers you, how do you feel? Very well.

When you don't have to do anything, what can you do? Whatever. So maybe nothing is just a state of no limits? Maybe when we die, we are nothing, so we can become anything new? Our everyday circle of life consist of being something, then falling asleep to be nothing, and waking up to be something again. And everyday we are a bit different, cause our brain is creating new connections between neurons, and deleting others. Maybe after death we continue this circle? We die to enter the void, and from the void comes new versions of reality? Just like our universe came from nothing!

It's hard to understand and accept, I know. But think again about our universe and how it came to be and why? If there was "nothing" before "something", then what determined what could arise and what could not? What could stop universe from being, if there is nothing? Nothing. There were no boundaries, no laws, no anything. So anything could have been created. ANYTHING can be created fro NOTHING, not in our current universe full of something already, but in universe that is NOTHING.

If you died and became nothing, how would you be sure that you would not become "something" again? You would have absolutely no certainty, because in "nothingness" there are no boundaries that would keep you there, and no laws that would forbid anything to arise. So yes, in essence – something arises from nothing. What are we now? In bodies, in material form, we are something.

We are like ready-made, written books. We have our minds, we have experiences, we have personalities and so on. And what can be written in an already written book? Not much. And what can be written in a blank book where there is nothing? Everything. Whatever. That is why nothingness means the possibility of the existence of anything, anything.

Maybe a year ago I came across a statement by a shaman, an alchemist on YouTube, who said that in order to get anything in life, you have to make room for it, because the universe abhors a vacuum, so when there is a vacuum in your life (a place for new things), these things come.

This is quite logical, because, for example, in order to be able to experience new experiences, you must first have time for it, so you have to give up some old habits. To start a new, healthy diet, you get rid of the old one. Before you start a new chapter, you close the old one.

So if you are struggling with some monotony, boredom, depression, sadness or a sense of hopelessness in life, the solution is (theoretically) simple. In practice, it's difficult, but doable – make a blank space in your life. Stop doing the things you do. Remove the apps that take up the most of your time. Look for new ones. Stop watching Netflix, or maybe you will start reading more in the place that appears (time saved)? Yes, it's logical that repeating the same activities every day gives the same results, so for example, every year I like to make some radical changes to make my life grow and change for the better – for example, I get rid of habits that consume the most of my time. And it works. New habits – a new you. Again, damn it, sounds like a cliché, but it's true. Seriously. Believe in nothing. Become nothing. Like nothing. DO NOTHING for a week. Then a new SOMETHING will appear. Because only when you pour the water out of the cup is there room for new water ;)

Exercise 22- Name 5 things that are obvious, but we rarely think about them or few people understand them.

Chapter 7: Good and Bad Pain

When you go to the gym and then you have soreness, you are not bothered or even too sad about the pain, because, firstly, you know its causes, and secondly, you know that it serves a purpose. This temporary pain is there to make your muscles grow, as well as your strength. First, as a result of the effort at the gym, microcracks have formed in their fibers, which your body will more than repair – and this is how the muscles grow. But man does not live by muscles alone, because in the gym the most valuable gain is the development of the psyche – self-discipline, resistance to pain and regularity.

A similar kind of "good pain" is probably felt by MMA fighters after winning a fight, because although their faces may be badly battered, they know that they made some money from it, had their moment of fame, gave a good show of martial arts, and above all – they showed a lot of courage by standing up to the fight, and then turned out to be better.

When I applied this kind of thinking to my life, finding any meaning and purpose in every pain and discomfort I endure, I was surprised at how much easier it is for me to get up for work, how much more efficiently and willingly I work, and above all – how much my level of happiness has increased. Getting out of bed is not pain, but discomfort that few people like. Still, there is a very big difference between discomfort that has a purpose and one that is senseless. In the first case, it takes little willpower to force oneself to do so, in the second – tons of it. And willpower is like a tank of fuel – it runs out. I try not to strain it too much, because otherwise, instead of buying pizza or doughnuts twice a week, I would do it twice a day.

That's why I've benefited greatly from a simple change in thinking about work. During the darkest, saddest time of my life, when I was financially desperate enough to work for a company that was going through all the nasty construction jobs no one else wanted, I was on the verge of being depressed, and maybe I already had it. When I got up for work, I wanted to cry, and on my way to work – to beat up anyone who was talking louder on the phone on the subway, disturbing my nap. I constantly wanted to sleep, I smoked cigarettes like crazy, I didn't pay attention at all to how and how much I ate, how many beers I drank, or how much weed I smoked. I did everything to escape from the sad reality.

One day, crawling in the basement, over the stones and sand, trying to squeeze under the ventilation duct to fill a rat hole with a lump of concrete (from which theoretically a rat could run out, straight into my face, so I was a little scared), ripping my back with the wire with which the thermal insulation of the ventilation ducts is wrapped, I thought:

- No, I'm fucking fed up! I'm about to quit this job in my cunt, I'll go to the Bieszczady Mountains and I won't come back. I have 50 Swedish kronor on my account, but I'll come up with something...

Then a second voice spoke:

- Don't be a cunt. Hehe.

And I listened to the latter, because a "real man" must bravely endure any suffering and not complain, right? Our ancestors endured the suffering of war, and you, Damian, feel like crying because of a few scratches from the soiled wire on your back, and a rat that didn't even have the courage to come out to meet you? Come on, wimp. Work because you planned a nice (I mean, expensive) vacation in Greece with your girlfriend, and then you fucked up half of your savings on stocks like a moron (the riskiest ones...), so... work, moron. This is your fate. Accept it. Don't complain!

But something was not right for me, I had an internal conflict all the time, because I remembered a quote from a boy who had been working in this company for 5 years:

- Come on, it's not that bad here! I don't know what you're all complaining about here!

And on the other hand, a quote from another who joked on my first day:

- Nice company, huh? Work here for half a year and get the fuck out of here as soon as possible, or you'll put down roots like him (he nodded at the one who didn't complain).

- And why aren't You running away? What are You doing here?- I asked, laughing

- I have to collect a few dozen more thousands for building my house, then I'll get the fuck out of here!

- Haha, I'm not saving for anything, so I can run away now!

But what kind of life is it when you don't save for anything? Not necessarily money. Think – When you have no expectations or plans for your future, what is the meaning of your every day and every suffering? Why live then? For today, and what! But my "today" was filled with hard, dirty, physical work. So I decided that the saying "carpe diem", meaning "seize the day", is absolutely not for me at the moment, because what am I supposed to seize? Rats, fuck?

I gritted my teeth and crawled on. Somehow I survived without a tear. A few days later, we had another mission – to kill the red ants in the kindergarten. First, we had to cut three stumps sticking out of the ground, in which they had nests, and then pour poison into the holes.

The boss, giving poison to an older guy I worked with, joked:

- Just hide it before you use it, so the ants don't see and expect, haha! *blink of an eye*

- Jojojoooo! Anders replied, with a serious face, nodding his head violently, as he used to do when he took orders.

When we cut the stumps, Anders told me to bring poison, so I did, walking with the bottle at my side, to which he blurted out with a frightened face:

- HIDE IT!

- Haha, yes, I forgot! – I said jokingly, pretending that I was hiding the poison behind my back, but after a while I walked with it normally again.

- WHAT ARE YOU DOING? HIDE IT BECAUSE THEY WILL SEE!

- But who? Kindergarten teachers? I asked, surprised by Anders' serious tone, suspecting that I had misunderstood his conversation with his boss, and that the Swedish words "ants" and "kindergarten teachers" might be similar or something. But they are not, I understood correctly.

-NO! ANTS!

As I understood English well, I stopped thinking: No, it's impossible that he isn't joking. He couldn't be THAT stupid, could he?

Yeah. He was. To euphemize, Anders was not endowed with a very high IQ, and to put it bluntly – he was fucking stupid as hell.

So I hid the poison behind me, and Anders wiped the sweat from his forehead with a clear look of relief on his face.

- A book could be written about this man and his funny moments! –I thought.

And then another thought came to my mind:

- And about me? Do I have an interesting life? What could be written in a book about my life? That I was sealing rat holes with concrete, working with Anders, hammering bathroom tiles with a small jackhammer, and when their shards fell on my face, I listened to an audiobook about successful people who stubbornly repeated that if I had a shitty job, I had to quit it and start doing what I loved? Or maybe I fucking love to plug rat holes?!

No. I hated every day at this job, but finally another thought came to my mind, somehow driven by the previous ones, about books:

- If I work like this all my life, a book about my miserable fate will contain no more than 5 pages - mainly filled with descriptions of pathetic complaints about dirty and hard work. But if I change it? If I achieve something? Maybe it doesn't matter where I am now, and where I WILL be if I finally start trying for a better fate? If I make my dreams come true (and the first one is to write a book), then I will have something to write about! But now I don't because I'm as boring as watching the grass grow! So how can I write something?! Whore!

Wait a minute! After all, the vast majority of writers don't write about their own lives, but create stories—detective stories, SF, romances, and so on—or use knowledge and thought to write something that influences people's thinking. So maybe the most important thing is not what kind of life you have, but what you have in your head? And what do I have in it? Shit! What should I write about? I know a lot of things, but I'm not advanced in any subject, so I won't write anything longer than 5 pages!

So it's time to learn! –I thought.

And I started addictively listening to audiobooks, mainly in the field of personal development, motivational, psychological and the like. Going to work, I no longer thought that I was going there to work like an ox just to survive, but to increase the resources of my mind while listening to audiobooks. Carrying heavy bags of rubble from the demolition from the third floor, I tried not to complain or think about the fact that my legs were about to get up my ass, but to listen to every word of the book and at the same time interpret them as best I could. To find wisdom in them or to counter them when they were inconsistent with the truth. Look for comparisons to your life in them, check their effectiveness.

And many times I paid for this lack of attention by almost falling down on the stairs, but whatever! I know that the lack of attention to what is "here and now" can be unhealthy, but on the other hand, at that moment it was really healthier for me to mentally escape from this extremely painful "here and now", into the world of books, because at least there was some sense in books.

When you suffer, find some meaning in it or turn it into something good – that's my slogan!

Just think of two hypothetical people, totally random:

One of them has been working in a horrible job for years, like Anders or something. Hypothetical Anders, of course. Then he dies. Anders... Ekhem, I mean a hypothetical man, he has no children. He left nothing behind in the world. He just died- poof! As if it had never existed! The world doesn't care, the world lives on. Wouldn't it be scary to be Anders? You mean, such a person? I am absolutely not saying that Anders' life has no meaning, because he did bring some added value to the world with his hard work, but nevertheless – it is a sad life and there is little significance in it.

Now the other person – he works in the same job, but every day he learns something new, writes down his thoughts and aspires to write a book. Doesn't her suffering make at least a little more sense? I don't want to compare myself to anyone, and I don't feel better than others, because I wrote something and others didn't (it's not my fault that I was born with such predispositions, nor Anders's fault that he was born without them, so I refrain from judging and judging), but with this example I want to show how I came out of the deepest mental shit, into which I was given the opportunity to fall – finding purpose and meaning in suffering.

Seriously, there's no fuck that you would survive torture if you knew that they torture you for drink, for example, because they know what you want to tell them anyway, and in the end they will kill you anyway. How much willpower would you have to survive it then? How much strength would you have to get through the suffering if you knew it would be eternal?

So now yes – first of all – know that no suffering is eternal. Secondly, find a higher purpose in your suffering, and you will really be surprised how much strength you have to get out of it. Look for meaning by force, like my drunk old needles in a haystack, but you're sure to find one somewhere. If I found mine – I, at that time hopeless, dust-stained, sad builder – anyone can.

Of course, this alone was not enough, because it took three years from that moment to find enough discipline and actually write a book, so in addition to having a goal, it is also worth slowly striving for it, but you know what I mean – it all starts with a change in thinking. Striving for a goal can even be slow like a slag that gets up with a hangover, but the goal itself – let it be somewhere. Change your thinking from pointless thinking to looking for purpose in everything. Even poop has its purpose, because after passing through the treatment plant it becomes fertilizer and eco vegetables will grow out of it – it's beautiful Even poop can be great. As long as you change your thinking about poop.

 This may sound like a silly cliché, but it's the purest truth. Just think about it – it is thinking that defines how you feel. Someone may feel good when a spider crawls on their hand, because they see in this spider only a miracle of nature, and someone else feels terrified because they see it as a threat.

Someone may feel great painting even the picture because they see it as a manifestation of their artistic nature, and someone else may feel insufficient, not very good and sad, even when they are painting a masterpiece because they don't believe in themselves. The brain is a hell of a complicated machine, but if you can find one simple thing in all these complications, I think it's the fact that

HOW YOU THINK, THAT'S HOW YOU FEEL!

Someone may feel good eating a donut because they think they deserved it after a grueling two-hour workout, and someone may feel guilty about it and tell themselves that all the training was now in vain (no, it didn't because you burned that donut before you ate it).

That's the whole philosophy. Feeling good depends on how you explain to yourself in your head everything you do, what people do— and so on. So it is worth having healthy and beneficial beliefs. But how to build them? Gaining inspiration and knowledge, and what!

Where are you supposed to get it from? And how am I supposed to know that? Get it where you like. I'm not here to tell you what to do. I can only show you the path that I am following to be a happier and happier person. You should not copy someone else's way, but you can successfully draw conclusions from it and guess what has a positive and negative effect on a person's life. So yes, changing your thinking works positively, as well as changing your socks, because the old ones already stink.

Exercise 23- List 5 types of pain or discomfort that you are able to endure or have already endured to achieve your goal

Chapter 8: Changing Negative to Positive

When I was about 12 years old, being a pretty fat kid, I was forced to do a few push-ups in PE, but I couldn't even do one. The whole class laughed terribly. When I got home, I cried for a long time because I hated my body – that fat son of a bitch who couldn't overcome gravity. He couldn't be better than others, and instead showed weakness. But I got pissed off then. This mental pain that that experience caused me has stayed with me forever and has definitely been turned into something good, because whenever I don't feel like exercising, and I planned to do it, I imagine a weak, fat Damian and think – oh no. I will not return to this place! No way.

And yes, they say it's harmful to be motivated by hatred and not love, but let's face it – nothing motivates more than a healthy dose of anger, because love is a feeling of peace, and when you're at peace, you don't want to go to training or make changes, go out of your comfort zone. But when you have anger, which is inherently a provoking feeling, you exercise like a beast.

This bad experience was one of the most valuable experiences of my life because it made me decide to lose weight. And not only did I decide, but I also knew that I would fucking do it. The measure was too much. Thanks to this, in two months I lost 8 kilograms and became a new, slightly better person, and then I started exercising regularly at the gym and felt better and better, becoming even a better person day by day. And you know what? It's great to have a beautiful body. This is really great, let's not fool ourselves. It's better than any doughnut or donut, or chocolate or ice cream, or kebab or pizza. But having a beautiful body isn't so great just because you're standing like a narcissist in front of a mirror and masturbating to your own reflection just because it's beautiful. No. The best thing about it is that you stand in front of the mirror and see that you have come to this body through hard work and willpower. You know you didn't have it before, and now you have it, and that says something—that you're willing to put in the FUCK of work to achieve something, so when you have it—your body is proof of your perseverance. That is why it is worth doing any sport. Not out of vanity and the desire to raise your ego, but to have living proof of how much you can do, how great a person you are and how much value hard work has. To have an example of your self-discipline in front of your eyes every day. So much.

The pain of being ridiculed, hating oneself or having an unattractive body can be successfully turned into one of the strongest motivations a person can have – the desire to be better than others and to prove those who laughed how wrong they were. This motivation has remained with me to this day, although 15 years have passed. I no longer consider the gym to be the most important aspect of my life, and I am constantly satisfied with my body, so I transferred this motivation to writing and I can promise you with a clear conscience that I will write as much as I can to become the best at it.

I learned on that fateful day that bad experiences can indeed be turned into something good. How can this help you change and change your reality? How can this change your thinking? Oh, very much, bull.

You see, many people feel so much stress and put so much pressure on themselves that when they want to change something, achieve something or tame their psyche, they lose their "flow" and live in constant fear, constantly asking themselves "What if I can't do it? What if I fall?" What if I stay in this hopeless state forever?"

Shit. You won't stay. There is no option. Every day something changes, we learn something every day, we try something new every day. To quote a classic: "Once or twice you failed, but that's no reason to give up! You have to go and fight!"

Because, you know, failures are the absolute norm. It's not so easy that if you want to lose weight, you will lose 10 kg in a week the first time. No. We all have to try to do something many times before we fully learn how to do it, so don't expect to get out of the pit in a week or even a month. Give yourself time. And that's it. Accept your failures.

Self-hatred can be a motivation, as I mentioned, but it shouldn't be sick and out of control. You don't have to whip yourself every day, relax. For example, I go to training when I have the strength to do it, but I don't feel like it – then I force myself. But if I don't have the strength or the desire – then I don't want to torture myself and force myself and I don't feel guilty that I don't train. So yes, I have some motivation to exercise, but it's not a sick obsession to exercise day after day. In the same way, for someone who wants to slowly start digging themselves out of the bottom of depression, I don't recommend that they put pressure on themselves, but rather that they use bad emotions to fuel themselves. And remember that these bad emotions cannot be denied or ignored. Bad feelings also need to be understood, accepted and worked through.

Exercise 24- List 5 situations in which you turned negative feelings into something positive

Feeling fear and stress is normal and sometimes even beneficial, but you can't live like this every day. You need to chill out. Smell the baboon, mordo. Take advantage of these bad vibes and bad energy and do something good. Focus on something good, then it will be easier, because everything is easier when you are not stressed. Even if you fall again and again, keep trying, like Najman. Many people who have come to me for dietary advice say something like: I've been trying my tenth diet and I've been struggling to lose weight for 2 years, and now, since I've been failing for so long, I doubt that I can do it at all! Help me to believe in myself again! Maybe I'm just doomed to be a walking cube of lard!?

No, you're not. If a programmer writes a program and doesn't work for two years, does it mean that the programmer will never write it? Well, no. He just needs to fix the mistakes. In the same way, a person who wants to lose weight will lose weight – if he notices his mistakes and changes something about it. Lack of success for 2 or even 5 years does not mean anything else than that you still have a chance for this success, and they are even getting bigger, because you are smarter or wiser.

It is the same in depression or any life breakdown. Have you been sitting down for 7 years and you think you're going to stay there? Bullshit. Life is paradoxical. Failures are not failures, but learning. Lack of success for 10 years does not reduce the chances of success, it increases. Every day, people are becoming wiser and more familiar with the situation they are in. Just like a newbie in a new job doesn't know anything about it at first and feels lost, but after a year he's already an ace in his company, so when you get depressed, you may think it's game over, after birds and so on – but it's quite the opposite. It can get better every day, AS long as you reach out for help and go to a psychologist and then start taking small steps.

So, if you had a child and saw that he fell off the bike ten times, learning to ride it, you wouldn't be mad at the child, because he falls because he can't do something – that's all. But he will learn. Nobody can live with depression either, but people learn it. So don't be mad at yourself if it doesn't work out for you at first. Don't feel stressed.

It's important when you fail and fall like child time and time again that you really LEARN from your mistakes. Something isn't working? Do it differently. Treat your mistakes as lessons. Let's assume that you have to fail about 1000 times to finally win against yourself and permanently change something in your psyche. Of course, this is just an example, and it's possible that trying to change your thinking will work after the first or 10 times.

But for example, let's say you keep making mistakes and have failed 950 times and you don't believe in yourself anymore. You know what? You only have to fail 50 times more, and you will eventually do it! Losing is good because every failure is your path to success! Each failure shows you a way in which something can't be done, so you can just lose 999 times, and that means you'll discover 999 wrong paths, so now you can just take that one right path! Be grateful, not stressed. It sounds like a cliché, but think logically: There are no endless options to try, there are a limited number of them. Every time you do anything, you're testing some new option for life. If 999 of them don't work and you feel like shit living the way you do, eventually, by force of things and the power of statistics, you'll find one thing that works.

It's like a scientist who tests 1000 different medicinal substances on himself, because he knows that with the power of statistics, at least a few will work. Don't be afraid to try (new habits, not ;) substances) and test new solutions, new books, new knowledge on yourself... and so on. This is how you come out of the current state – doing something new. By doing the same as before, you will achieve the same results as before. New steps = new results.

Exercise 25 – List 5 situations in which it is easiest for you to control your mind, negative thoughts or emotions

Chapter 9: Expectations

Imagine that you have been working as a septic tank for 10 years. Your work is thankless, dirty and poorly paid. You barely have enough for bread. You don't have a wife, because no one would want to be with a person who stinks like that, I'm sorry. You have dirty nails that never want to wash you, and the peak of your entertainment is staring at the TV after work. You sleep on a leaky mattress, eat sandwiches with mortadella (without even margarine), and the only vegetable you eat is ketchup. Suddenly... Your life is changing! Some businessmen come to you and say:

- Hey, you! You're wasting yourself! Come work for us, you will invest in the stock market!

-I? What are you! I don't know anything about it!

- We will teach you everything! We know you had an A in math in school. IQ 105. Simply. Come. Just wash yourself.

- Okay, thanks!

And from that day on, you've been working as a stockbroker, so you're making really good money. Your friends are going to lunch at a respectable, good restaurant, and you pull out a good classic – a dry mortadella sandwich – so they start laughing. In addition, all the men have expensive watches and shirts, and you - a "wife-beater" tank top and shorts with Donald Duck with a beak in a known place. And everyone drives some nice cars, and you came by bus.

"Have you seen the new one?" Where did he get off from, haha!- say his colleagues from work.

- Hey, I hear you! I'm standing right next to you!- you answer.

- Oh, sorry, new. After all, we like you and we would never gossip about you! Come to lunch with us, just dress like a human!

So you start going to a good restaurant with them, and your taste buds explode with a wave of sensations, experiencing culinary delight and a bouquet of sophisticated flavors that they did not know before. At first you have a problem with using cutlery, but eating soup with your hands is a bad idea, so you learn to use a spoon and somehow make it.

For the next 10 years, you go to this job. The pleasures of a rich life gave you a lot of joy at first, because they were something new, but after a while they became the norm. But there is a small problem...

- Get up, Czesiu! Hear?! – your boss wakes you up.

-What? – you ask in shock.

"Come on, you sewer rat!" You came to work drunk again and let it go. You slept so deeply that we couldn't wake you up. We were already afraid that you were in a different world, hehe.

-I 've been... I... I was in another world!

- Oh Czesiu, Czesiu... you'd better end this vodka...

-But...

It turns out that it was just a dream. You come back home – again dirty, again smelly, again eating a sandwich with mortadella – but this sandwich doesn't taste like it used to. It tastes terrible. Why? Because you have raised expectations. Your own stench also smells horribly, because you got used to the pleasant smell of perfume on your shirt, and yet – the stench of rags again. Your life, although it sucked, was bearable, because you get used to everything, seriously. And now – it's unbearable, because you've experienced a better life and you have much, much more expectations. You compare yourself to stock market meclairs and feel like a Pole-worm except that you do a much less paid job. And your senses, already accustomed to very high levels of pleasure, are not able to enjoy small pleasures as they used to.

So, in order to be happy, do you have to have the lowest expectations and try as little as possible? Absolutely not. I once saw a comment from a frustrated guy on TT:

- Tera te baby is mayo who knows what expectations! Earn more than 5 thousand per month, eat healthy, don't drink every day... drama.

Well, these expectations are really very big. However, it seems to me that it is healthy to have any, because if "women" did not expect at least such a minimum from a "peasant", they would enter into relationships with every, even the most neglected bumbler, and men would have no motivation to take care of themselves, because let's face it – for many guys the basic and most subconscious, evolutionarily programmed motivation to take care of themselves is to increase the chances of finding a partner and procreation. So it's very good to have expectations! And not only towards ourselves, but also towards others. The problem is that many have inadequate expectations. For example, a woman who doesn't take care of herself, eats unhealthily, earns little, isn't a good mother, smokes cigarettes and is empty as a shoe and boring, wants to find a guy who drives a Porshe, has 20 hobbies and is a bodybuilder. Or a guy who drinks 10 beers a day, goes out to bars with his friends, expects a woman to stop going out to parties and only sit at home, because a woman is not allowed to risk ever cheating on him, or God forbid to talk to other guys at all.

And the same applies to life – each of us should have some healthy expectations, because without them we would agree to anything. In embarrassing companies with embarrassingly low hourly rates, in which I had the opportunity to work, this was the problem of most people – they agreed to the worst shit, just to have this relatively normal paycheck, And they never even thought that there are companies where the boss pays better, but for doing less tiring, cleaner, more decent work. It can be similar in toxic relationships, where two people are with each other not out of love, but out of fear that they will never find someone better, or no one at all, because they have toxic or weak personalities themselves, so they stick to the worst, although the only option that they think they have left – a toxic relationship and lowering their expectations of the person, with which they are.

My fiancée immediately tells me when, in her opinion, I reach for beer too often and I'm not mad at her about it, on the contrary – I'm glad that she has this vigilance, because you don't always see on your own when you get into an addiction. I've never had problems with alcohol and I'm a great control over this aspect of life, but who knows? Maybe I would have had fewer and fewer chances to live in sobriety if it weren't for its reminders? Maybe the percentage of alcoholism in Poland would drop by at least 10% if women were not afraid to tell their husbands that in their opinion they drink too often, or by 99% less if men had the balls to admit that they have a problem when they actually have one? Especially with such a dangerous and harmful substance as alcohol, where the line between a daily beer for pleasure, as a reward, and addiction is thin.

So you can say that my fiancée has normal expectations of me, because not falling into alcoholism is the norm, and alcoholism is a pathology (a state of deviation from the norm) that should be avoided. If you allow your other half to drink every day, think about what her expectations of yourself are so low that she does it to herself, and above all – why are YOUR expectations so low that you don't pay attention to her, you just agree to it?

The point is that you MUST NOT agree to everything that is worst, because then you will be the worst yourself and you will live like a cesspool, so have expectations as much as possible. But think about the fact that on the other hand, many, many people have unrealistic expectations about life.

Three hundred years ago, even kings could dream of such luxuries as a hot shower, the Internet, unlimited access to books and movies, a mobile device for communicating with the world in their pocket, a self-riding horse (i.e. a car) and other such things. We have it today. Only so much and AS much. When was the last time you were grateful for this? I thank you for that every day. Because it's really a lot.

Exercise 26- List at least 5 situations in which you think people expect too much. Understand that you don't have to be perfect all the time, because people's expectations are not a good system for evaluating yourself

Chapter 10: Brain Hygiene

Once, in one of the largest stock exchange halls on Wall Street, an unusual investor appeared – a chimpanzee named Charlie. It was part of an experiment to prove how random choices affect investment results. Charlie was not familiar with technical analysis, forecasts or trends. Charli knew nothing about the stock market, seriously. Because Charlie was a fucking monkey. Instead, he threw darts at the list of companies, choosing his "investments" in a completely random way.

To everyone's surprise, Charlie's wallet was doing great. Not only did it outperform the average investor, but it also outperformed top brokers. In the first quarter, its rate of return was 20%, while elite brokers barely pulled out 5%. The media quickly gave him the title "Banana Buffett".

The brokers were furious. "How is it possible that this furry amateur is better than me, a Harvard man?!" one of them shouted, grabbing his head. Others tried to look for a conspiracy, claiming that Charlie must have inside information (although this was quite difficult to imagine). Still others pissed in Charlie's coffee and had a burp when he drank it, and he had a burp because he knew it, but he didn't care.

Over time, the frustration turned into destructive habits. One broker started to overdo expensive bourbon, another invested his life savings in bitcoin at the top of the bubble, hoping to make up for the losses. One even dropped everything and decided to breed alpacas in Peru, convinced that he would never match Charlie's genius.

The experiment lasted a year. Charlie still had better results than most experts. At the end of the study, his tutor gave a short speech:

"Charlie is not a genius. What you see is the force of randomness. Sometimes we try too hard to anticipate the unpredictable instead of accepting that certain things are out of our control."

Moral? Life, just like the stock market, is full of coincidences and chaos. Perhaps it is sometimes worth putting aside the obsession with control and accepting what fate brings. And if you can't... you can always try throwing darts like Charlie. Or to in someone's coffee.

But seriously – seriously many things cannot be changed in life. Play with the cards that fate has dealt to you. Sorry, you have no choice. The sooner you understand this and start living in accordance with it, the better.

Each of us got a different brain – me like this, you like that. Mine is good at writing and remembering interesting facts about the human body, but he has two left hands and gets lost even in his own city, plus he is extremely easily distracted. I'm not complaining that I have such a brain that can't concentrate, I just use the one I have.

In addition, when I'm tired or overstimulated, I get distracted even more easily, and this is probably due to the excess of dopamine, which is harmful to me, so I have to take care of a good night's sleep, a reasonably good diet and control the level of stimulants so as not to mess up my brain even more.

Exercise 27- List at least 5 of your strengths.

Every brain degrades with age. Of course, this happens faster in people who abuse alcohol or drugs. But not only. As a result of stress, trauma, poor sleep quality, environmental toxins, or deficiencies of various substances – neurons can die. And it's very easy to destroy them, but not so easy to rebuild. So scientists have been wondering for years – how to keep the brain fit for many years? How does the structure of this organ affect our well-being, memory or personality? What makes us smarter, and what makes us stupid?

If I found a goldfish, or a dying in a lamp, or anything else that grants wishes, one of them would be to know all the secrets of the human brain, to find out what is destroying it, and how to at least slow it down. Then I would discover a cure not only for dementia and depression, but maybe even schizophrenia, Parkinson's syndrome, multiple sclerosis... and many more.

If you were to ask a really good mechanic how a car's engine works, they would probably explain to you its structure and all the processes that take place there, from A to Z.

If you asked a neurologist how the human brain works, the doctor could tell you about the general principles of its operation, but he would not explain everything – because no one knows everything about the brain yet. It's such a fiendishly complicated machine that we're still in the phase of experimenting on it. Treating depression is not a certainty – no one will give you a drug that will work 100%. You can get a drug that works harder, but you can also get one that won't help you. This does not mean that you should give up trying to treat it, but rather that you should maintain a minimum of patience and understanding, because after all, an ineffective drug can be replaced with another, until you finally find one that works very well.

Despite everything, depression is still a mystery. We guess that it is caused by a deficiency of serotonin, which is known as the happiness hormone. But why doesn't raising serotonin levels in everyone and immediately cure depression?

Serotonin is like a key, and for it to work, it has to fit into a keyhole. Such holes are receptors in the brain. Each hormone has its own specific receptors, and if they are broken, even a colossal amount of serotonin will not help you. Therefore, for example, taking MDMA (a drug also known as Ecstasy) is not a good idea, because although it causes a rapid increase in serotonin levels, the brain flooded with this hormone loses a lot of receptors. It's like trying to squeeze two keys into one hole at a time. The hole pushes and breaks down, so it is unusable later. And while a one-time use of MDMA is unlikely to leave significant changes in your brain, overusing it for years could completely devastate you.

And it's exactly the same with alcohol. Alcohol imitates GABA (a calming hormone) and that's why we feel so great after it. Unfortunately, we have strong evidence that shows that GABA receptors are very susceptible to destruction when overactivated. Each dose of alcohol kills some of these receptors. Especially high and regular doses.

But it turns out that not only stimulants destroy our brains. Many substances in our diet have a pro-inflammatory effect, and inflammation also directly increases the risk of depression, dementia or other diseases. Anti-inflammatory foods, on the other hand, generally show an inverse correlation with depression. Each serving of fruit or vegetables a day (most of which are anti-inflammatory) reduces the risk of depression by 3%.

It doesn't seem like much, but every small brick added to the well-being of your brain can decide in the future whether you will be happy or not.

Olive oil also has a strong anti-inflammatory effect. It is (next to omega-3 fatty acids) one of the healthiest foods for the brain. Why? Guess what the myelin sheaths of nerves are made of, i.e. their electrical insulation? Omega-9 acids, i.e. those that olive oil has the most.

It is also likely that inflammation, even a slight but long-lasting one, promotes the death of receptors. So maybe the secret to preventing depression is simply to flood the brain with good fuel, just as flooding the engine with good oil promotes its lifespan?

Why is it rarely mentioned and why do few people pay attention to it?

First of all, we tend to think in binary terms, i.e. either A or B.

So when someone asked you what you think the cause of depression is, you'd probably say it's childhood traumas, negative thoughts, stress—and so on. Everything mental.

A psychologist will certainly agree with you, but a dietician may think that the cause of depression is precisely what you flood your brain with – that is, the food you eat.

But the brain is so complicated that you can't just choose one of these answers and think you've discovered revealed truth, the one, the only one, and the absolute.

Depression is probably a combination of both. It has biological and mental causes. We never know which ones are more important, and it probably varies from person to person. People focus so much on mental causes that they forget about biological causes—and vice versa.

We know that there are people who are less stressed than others in certain situations, and stress does not affect them so negatively. We say that they are mentally strong, self-confident, resilient... But where does this strength come from? Where does their peace of mind come from?

Maybe it is due to the structure of their brains? Maybe they won the genetic lottery and have twice as many serotonin receptors as you or me? Maybe they have a lot more GABA? Or maybe they just eat something every day that has a beneficial effect on the brain, but they don't even know it?

We are literally made of what we eat, because our body obtains all the building blocks from food. So if you eat sweets every day, bizarre amounts of saturated fat (they can be pro-inflammatory) or spread a lot of margarine on bread (also pro-inflammatory), and avoid vegetables, scientifically and statistically speaking, you have a much higher chance of depression than someone who eats olive oil and a lot of vegetables every day.

Of course, the fact that someone eats super healthy is no guarantee of maintaining mental health. Certain traumas and certain amounts of stress or negativity cannot be withstood by any brain, no matter how much you take care of it. But it's better to have a stronger brain than a weaker one, right?

Hence, I appeal to everyone who reads this – try to take care of your mental hygiene and the condition of your brain. No one has the perfect motivation or ideal circumstances to eat healthy always and everywhere, but that doesn't mean we're helpless in the face of life.

When I want a beer, but I don't meet my friends – I don't drink beer. I don't drink alone, because it's pointless and unnecessary. When I choose an oil in the store, it is always olive oil. When I'm deciding whether to eat chips with cream-based garlic dip or sweet potato fries with guacamole dip, I might even fail 4 out of 5 and eat chips, but 1 out of 5 I'll choose guacamole, and who knows? Maybe this one, small decision will allow me to enjoy a fit brain at least 10 days longer?

If you had to choose between having dementia today or in 10 days, what would you choose? Of course, you'd rather postpone this sentence just a little, right?

Realize that dementia is a real scourge of the 21st century, just like depression.

So maybe life consists of such small decisions. And maybe we are only human, and our appetite is rather not conducive to making the right and healthy ones – it's normal. There is nothing to blame. EVERYONE eats something unhealthy from time to time and EVERYONE has their weaknesses.

But knowing how high the stakes (your mental health) are, maybe you'll remind yourself of it from time to time and at least 20% of the time choose something healthier?

Because the key to health, I suppose, is knowledge. Becoming aware of how the brain works and why it is worth supporting it in this activity.

I think people care more about their homes, phones and cars than their brains.

Let's change that. Let's promote brain hygiene, because we have nothing more valuable than our brains.

In a world where everyone is busy, stressed, tired, and prone to addiction, 99% of us don't even have the opportunity to have a perfect, healthy diet.

But we absolutely don't have to be perfect. We don't have to do anything. However, we CAN, step by step, become a little better and inspire others to do the same. I think it's damn important. That's why I'm writing about it. And that's why a book that is set in the world of the future and science fiction should really make us think and think about it – if the main character feels so many negative emotions because of a stupid chip, which is a small thing affecting his brain, maybe we ourselves have such things in our own brains? Maybe every substance we eat builds or destroys our sense of happiness in a greater or lesser way? Maybe every thought or emotion that appears in us is not a coincidence, but what we build our brains from?

And of course, this is just a biological perspective. That's not all. Brains, in addition to all this physical, chemical tangle of neurons, are also made of thoughts and emotions. Every thought and emoxy you repeat every day builds new connections in your brain.

Complaining about life for one day won't do you anything, but complaining 365 days a year will build your brain in such a way that negativity becomes obvious.

Therefore, brain hygiene is not only about taking care of our diet, but also about how and what we think about. What we surround ourselves with, what emotions we fall into and give them control over our lives. Think about it.

And while we're on the subject of hygiene, I'll tell you the name of the substance I wrote about at the beginning – the one that inhibits the production of adrenaline and can be beneficial for the brain – it's CBD.

Exercise 28 – List at least 5 situations where you can easily choose something healthier instead of unhealthy

Chapter 11: Ants

Can ants be smarter than us in some respects?

Absolutely. How! Look at what these insects do when someone destroys their anthill. Of course, don't do this to them, just imagine it!

They will try to rebuild their home. If someone destroys it again and again, they will eventually find a better place to build it, but they will never stop doing it because that's how they're programmed. And when Anders puts poison in their anthill (so that they can't see), maybe they won't die right away, but run away and build a house somewhere else? They will not fall into alcoholism and break down, but will continue to work and take care of the queen. Ants do not think and do not despair, they just live. Maybe we should also learn to simply live with failures and unfavor of fate, not thinking about them for too long, and focusing on what we can influence? We have the greatest influence on ourselves and our brains, like something.

You could say that your body is like an anthill for an ant, because you live in it. And daily habits can build a healthier and slimmer body, or destroy it, or a healthier and happier psyche, or destroy it. It's no reason to be ashamed when you "let yourself go" a bit, because each of us has worse and better periods in life. Everyone sometimes neglects one aspect of their life because they have to focus on another. Of the two evils, it's better to neglect your body a little (because you can always rebuild it relatively quickly, of course, if you haven't overdone it yet and you don't have some incurable disease because of it), than to destroy yourself financially to the level where you lose everything and don't know how to survive another day, or destroy your relationship with your family. Sure, it's sad when you lose your shape, but you have to understand that as long as you're alive and you're not bedridden or toileted by illness, there's no tragedy.

There is not a single person who succeeds after success in life, every time, in every field. The fact that sometimes your "home" is weakened by bad habits does not mean that you can no longer do anything about it and you should give up. That's what many people think. Failures are a reason for them to abandon all efforts and consider themselves too weak. But why believe in such harmful nonsense? You're not weak, unless you put such a badge in your own head.

And isn't it better, instead, to consider failures as lessons and the natural course of things, so after each failure try again until you finally succeed? If there is such a thing as failure at all. It is possible that life consists of cycles, such as seasons. Sometimes you lose weight, sometimes you gain weight – and there's nothing wrong with that! Absolutely nothing! Don't believe in the false image of perfection that social media tries to impose on you. Of course, there are people with very good habits, like athletes, but even they lose them when, for example, an injury comes and then they have to rebuild their form. Besides, no one pays you to stay in shape all year round, so you just don't feel compulsive. Because there is no such compulsion!

A destroyed anthill doesn't mean you can't repair it anymore. On the contrary! The more anthill has been destroyed, the greater the potential for reconstruction, so you have a much better chance of transforming your body than someone who has been exercising for years and will find it rather difficult to build another kilogram of muscle or burn another piece of fat.

Being a dietitian means having knowledge and sharing it with others, and, if possible, passing on to patients what I have tested on myself and know that it works. And since I have periods of gaining weight and losing weight all the time, I know a lot!

And the title of dietician will by no means make me have a perfect body! I'll say more – I'm far from perfect, but I still like my body and only when I cross some visual limit of attractiveness in my head, I start the weight loss process. I want to do more when I know that there is a lot to do, so the pride in completing the task will also be high. I don't break down when I see a hundred or so kilograms on the scale in winter, because I know that from now on I'm losing weight – and that's it. It's a nice challenge. For me, it's not a failure to be slightly fatter than the ideal norm. I like to eat, I also like to have a nice body, and I like to have this and that even more. Who doesn't? The so-called – have your cake and eat it too. The wolf is full and the sheep is whole. A wolf is your appetite for tasty food, a sheep is your body, demanding to lose a few unnecessary kilograms. You can have both when you don't live like a slave to your own belief in failure (by the way, you don't see successes anymore?), and you just finally realize that gaining weight and losing weight was, is and will be natural, just like being down and being happy. You can stay in shape for as long as possible, but if you gain weight – no loss. Lose weight again. And if you are depressed – don't worry, it is not a permanent state. People come out of it. Seriously.

If I already eat a lot and my body enjoys the goodness, I can lose it later. Why should I break down and why should I believe that I will fail? Every time I believe that it will succeed, it succeeds. It is logical that it is better to believe in yourself than not to believe. It's the same with my psyche – when I get tired to the point that I'm as tired as a horse after a western, I rest for a few weeks. The English word for someone depressed – depressed – in pronunciation is "dip-rest", the same as deep rest, so maybe depression is a period of deep rest that occurs when we are already hellishly tired of it all? Maybe then you just have to give yourself time?

No one has ever documented a single ant that breaks down, sits by the ruins of an anthill, smokes a cigarette, grabs its head with its legs, calls its ant friend and complains – oh, I'm no good! Someone destroyed my anthill again! Ants don't do this because they don't have the slightest idea in their insect brain of what failure is, so they don't recognize it. But they know perfectly well how to build, so they do it. Yes, buddy - your psyche is such an anthill.

Exercise 29- List 5 situations where he did not give up despite failures

Chapter 12 – I want to want.

Are you poor? So apparently you don't want to be rich, because if you wanted hard enough, you'd definitely find a way!

Are you overweight? So apparently you don't care that much about a healthy and beautiful body, because if you did, you would finally get to work! – at least that's what some "motivators" say, who think that if they criticize you and call you lazy, something will finally work in you, and suddenly you will start working more, harder, smarter – becoming an ideal in every area of life. After all, "if you want it, you can do it", right? If you really want something, you will find a way – yes, but very often there are so many ways to get something, and there are so many things to get in life that we don't know what we want. Desires are also variable. The motivation is not constant, but it fluctuates.

Some people think that achieving success in any area of life, getting out of depression or overcoming their weaknesses is only due to motivation. They say they'll start going to the gym, but not today! Tomorrow? Day after tomorrow? You know... As soon as they feel like it! But when do they feel like it and why should they want to do it at all? They don't know that anymore!

The will, if it is really very strong, makes you overcome various obstacles on the way to your goal with greater ease than someone who does not have this desire. If you have a very strong desire to eat a candy bar, you will go to the store to eat it, even if it rains, winds and hail. And if the desire is minimal – you will not move from the couch, or you will settle for bread with sugar. So it's quite important to have willingness, but a person does not live by willingness alone. But where did the desire come from? How to make you want to when you don't want to? Good question. It seems to me that it is worth having a vision in your head, because it drives you to act, just like the vision of having gold drives you to dig to get it. If you "want something", convince yourself that it is worth having and that you can have it. Imagine having it and enjoy it, but don't just daydream.

Other motives (those a little more clever and familiar with psychology) claim that motivation is to drink water. You shouldn't rely on it, and you can even throw this word out of your vocabulary at all. Human desires and motivations are unreliable and unstable, like Aunt Krysia's motivation to stick to the cabbage diet. Anyone who has ever had a New Year's resolution and kept it for a week knows that, hehe. The fact that today you want to eat and exercise healthily (because, for example, it's a new year and you assume – new year, new me!), absolutely doesn't mean that tomorrow you will also want to do so, does it? So what should you rely on? On self-discipline and self-control, of course. And it can be made, but it takes a lot of time. And nowhere does it say that if you develop the discipline to go to the gym, you will also have the discipline to eat healthier, save money or study in your free time. I used to think that was how it worked, and since I had the discipline to train, I should also be able to write books for eight hours a day, right? Well, no. I expected god knows what from myself (like Janusz from the Polish team playing a match against Germany) and many times I disappointed myself, severely and painfully. Now, wiser (like every Pole after a loss), I can tell you that you shouldn't expect too much from yourself. Example? You want to get out of depression, but you don't do it for months, you just continue to lie in bed and rot. So what? Shit, don't blame yourself. It wasn't you who fucked it up, it was your brain. There is absolutely no reason to blame yourself for anything. It is important to try until it works, because it will come out one day. Another example – you were supposed to stick to your diet and eat 1500 kcal a day, but one day you were tired, stressed and so on, and it happened – you ate a whole pizza and a bucket of ice cream. So what? Shit. You can still stick to your diet, because one day doesn't have to ruin your whole life. Another situation in the life of a typical person – you wanted to go on vacation and you had to save 10 thousand in a fixed time for this purpose, and you only saved 5. What to do? Cry and give up on plans? Well, no. Keep putting it off and that's it.

I often have high expectations for writing and plan to write 10 pages on a given day, and it turns out that I have only written 3. And what? Shit. And so I fall asleep, affirming gratitude to myself, because the average person didn't write a single page on a given day. In fact, most people don't even read every day. So I have a reason to be proud and you probably also have your reasons, which you will find if you try.

Writing is not easy, even if I have ideas for future books. I don't have inspiration every day. So my fiancée tells me not to force myself and wait until I have the inspiration. Apparently, he wants to spare me suffering and does not want me to do something against myself, but I have a slightly different opinion on this subject. In fact, I don't rely on motivation or inspiration, I just force myself. And that's it. There is no other option. Someone may think that writing is torture, but intensive training also causes some discomfort, and yet after completing it, we feel like young gods. So maybe in life you shouldn't even expect everything to go smoothly, but have the balls to face some obstacles thrown at your feet, like your great-great-great-grandfather, who supposedly went to school 150 kilometers a day and then grew wheat for 28 hours a day. But more seriously – people used to work more and were tougher, so if they could work 12 hours a day, why does so much work seem like slavery and torture to us? Because first of all – we are used to it, like someone who has slept on a soft bed all their life and then wants to switch to sleeping on boards. Secondly, most of us don't really like our work and don't see any point in it, and if we did something we like, we wouldn't mind overtime. It is not said that your great-great-ancestors loved growing wheat, but they HAD to do it to survive. You, today, theoretically – you don't have to do anything, you can do everything. You choose to work alone. You choose your paths of life, and there are hundreds (or even dozens) of them to choose from....

Someone who is a fanatic of silkworm breeding could do it after work and derive satisfaction from it, and someone who likes to write will also find time for it after work, because in the 21st century we work ONLY 8 hours a day. People complain that work is a form of slavery, but haven't they imposed such slavery on themselves, choosing a job they don't like, instead of developing and gaining better competences?

I'm not going to lie – I feel proud when I write. Reading develops because it allows us to absorb new information, but writing develops even more strongly because it extracts and helps to process the information we already have. If writing were my job, I would become the happiest man on Earth, although just starting to write makes my brain rebel and say, come on, man! Lie down, play games! In this aspect, my brain is not my friend, but my enemy. I have to control this damn jelly to make it want to do anything at all. And once I've gotten through the first half hour of writing, I'm slowly starting to get going, even if my brain doesn't want to cooperate at the moment, so instead of sending information like a modern supercomputer, it spews out words more or less at the speed of a chimpanzee typing random letters and then having to delete half of them because they don't make sense.

When I don't want to go to work because I just want to sleep longer, I go there anyway. I have to use self-control. And all in all, I get some benefit from it, because I have a little more money, right? So if I can force myself to work, maybe I can force myself to do anything, but I need to have a clear vision of the benefits that I will achieve thanks to it?

So I use a similar logic when writing, when going to the gym... And that's it, because in other areas of life I don't have much self-control at all.

It's just that sometimes in life you have to force yourself, but when you don't have the strength to force yourself to do many things at once, force yourself only to do what is most important. Force yourself to take small steps.

Self-control is extremely important because we live in a world that is somehow not conducive to good health and well-being, because it constantly puts us to the test. You walk next to the bakery, you are hungry, and the smell of a doughnut reaches your nose. Will you buy it, or will you go further to the vegetable stall, where you will buy celery and then eat it with tears in your eyes while your co-workers eat doughnuts and laugh at you? This is one of such attempts. We have hundreds of delicious products and eating each of them, every day, would inevitably end up with obesity, so naturally each of us has to resist it somehow, choosing what is relatively healthy.

You're drunk as a bale and some inconspicuous-looking guy in a bar told you that you look like Peter Griffin from "Family Guy", which offended your male ego in an obvious and shameful way, so you're wondering whether to beat this scoundrel or laugh about it and skip the matter? This is one of the tests. The aggression that arises in us when someone criticizes us can be dangerous and make you get into a fight with someone crazy who, instead of using his fists, will use a chair, a bottle or a knife. Or with someone who has practiced kicboxing and kicks you in the head so hard that you fall unconscious and smash your head. That is why anger is not a good advisor, and controlling it is another manifestation of emotional maturity and an important feature of a modern man, which should be nurtured like Aunt Krysia her feet for two hours before she goes for spa treatments, so she wants to wipe off the skin accumulated over decades on her heels, which makes her 2 cm taller and has skin as rough as a dinosaur.

Your wife asks you to give her the salt shaker at dinner. Will you give it or use unflattering words to express your general frustration with life, saying that your lover wasted 20 years of your life? This is another test. Maybe for some it is easy to win, because they are happy in their relationship and love their wife, but for others – what a difficult challenge it is not to say something unpleasant to a person with whom you have spent half of your life. Being kind and creating good relationships pays off, because it leads to happiness. Creating wars or a personal war in one's own home is a way to tarnish one's nerves, like the strings of a guitar that a drunken postman tugged furiously, wanting to prove that he can play it, but he can't.

A lot of things in your life depend on how much you control yourself and your wants and needs. Remember, however, that life does not have to and should not be a fight with yourself, and self-control is not always the result of forcing yourself. After a while, the workout you force yourself to do becomes a habit, so you don't have to force yourself anymore. The first two weeks can be hard, but life doesn't have to be hard.

Also, remember not to fall into the trap of thinking typical for many people – they think that if they develop their self-discipline in one area, it will automatically translate into all other areas of life. For example:

- I've been going to the gym for five years.

-Woow! Man, you have a strong psyche!

- Strong as hell. When I see a doughnut, I don't even feel tempted to eat it anymore! I am a master of mastering my own psyche, I make it work for me, not me for it. I am a demigod. A living legend!

-Seriously?! Wow! Impressive! The gym has made you a beast, not only physically, but mentally! And what does your self-control look like when you control your anger outbursts?

-Well, I can't do that yet... I explode often, for any reason. As soon as something irritates me, I feel like biting my elbow or shuffling my heel on the carpet.

-Interesting... and what does your financial discipline look like?

-Well, I don't have it either. I spend money thoughtlessly and always borrow it from friends at the end of the month...

-Hmm... And getting up in the morning to work? Do you do it without any problem?

-No! I have to force myself, and getting out of bed requires me to turn off at least five snooze alarms.

-Endorsement... And what about self-control in the case of mastering risky behaviors, such as losing money on slot machines?

-Oh, I'm lying here too, squealing! Whenever I'm drunk, I lose at least a thousand at slot machines!

-So you don't have as much self-control as you think...

-Bullshit! I have a lot of self-control! I just want to do some things and others... no.

-So if you want to go to the gym, you don't use self-control to do it, but willingness. If you didn't feel like it, and you went there anyway, then you would use self-control.

-Bullshit! You don't know anything about the human psyche! My favorite bald coach from TikTok, who promotes toxic masculinity and harmful thinking patterns, said that self-control gained in the gym will help me in literally every area of my life!

- Maybe he was just wrong? As in many other matters... Like many pompous quivers who don't practice the art of psychology or motivation, but just say something theoretically cool, in a cool way, so they win naïve fans (usually 17-year-old boys who, entering the period of manhood, also want to be fit and rich), but despite this, they just... Fuck pharmacies?

-Impossible!

Or maybe coke? When for years of going to the gym and looking only a little better than the average person I didn't see much effect, I cruelly admired bodybuilders who have the discipline to train for hours and stick to a strict diet every day. I was convinced that they were gods in every area of life, and yet they were not. They just like the gym so much that they will do anything for it, but they can still struggle with problems in other spheres – just like all of us. Elon Musk, although he is a genius, does not have a wife, because he did not even have time for her. When he invited his ex to the hotel (supposedly to talk about rockets and space), and she hoped for a hookup, Musk actually preferred to talk about space, such a fanatic he is. Fanatics of one field achieve success in it, but they do not have to be perfect. Nobody has to be perfect at everything, but it's worth becoming better than you were a year ago. Albert Einstein was also a genius, but he treated his wife as a private servant. He lacked the desire to create a healthy, happy relationship with someone.

And how to live here? Trust your willingness, or maybe discipline? Develop at the gym or write books?

How about ... Trust nothing and no one? Forget it. Do nothing, no matter if you want to or not! What a wonderful way to live! Just think – totally stress-free, no tension, no stress. Sit on the couch, watch TV, and don't try to do anything if you really don't have to! It will be a simple, loose life. What more could you want? You don't want to go to work, then don't go. You will become homeless after a month, but whatever.

Okay, and more seriously – maybe instead of trusting the apparent wisdom of experts from the Internet (including me), trust what you check on yourself and know that it works? Just keep trying new things. Since 90% of small businesses fail, maybe you just have to fail 9 times to succeed once? Since most people can't lose weight and give themselves after the fifth attempt, maybe six attempts would be enough for them, because the sixth one will work? By checking something new every time, you will eventually come across a good solution. Life offers so many opportunities that it is a pity not to take advantage of them. If someone tells me that they don't have a hobby, I usually see a simple solution for such a person – try new things, you'll find it! However, people sometimes do not want to search, which is a pity. Who seek, will find. It's the same when building new habits, discipline or a greater sense of happiness – not everything works for everyone, so it's normal when something goes wrong. Don't expect success right away and don't put pressure on yourself to become a millionaire in a week. Change only what can be changed at the moment. Do not do it impetuously and greedily, but using the snail method. Or a turtle. Or a baby learning to walk. Whatever you prefer.

Exercise 30 – List 5 situations where you could gradually change your life in small steps

Chapter 13: Ways

"Your life will never change until you change.

Or, in a different version, until you change what you do every day"

Because, as Albert Einstein himself said, only a madman would do the same thing over and over again, but expect different, new results.

No one has yet invented a recipe for a perfect life – which is a pity. We also don't have a recipe for happiness, curing depression, good relationships with others, or financial success. But that doesn't mean these things are unattainable. They are simply complicated and require rehearsals. So you won't get a ready-made recipe from anyone, but you can create your own recipe for a cake called well-being, if you experiment and try new things, like aunt Kryisia, who, bored with apple pie, tried to bake karpatka, but it turned out to be a nook. Then the second and the third and the tenth, but the eleventh time she succeeded.

Life is not like a cake, so a recipe from the Internet is unlikely to work.

If someone claims to know such a recipe – they probably want to get money from you and sell you some bullshit.

By the way – I encourage you to buy my two previous books, in which I described one hundred percent and reliable and one hundred percent effective ways for perfect, superhuman self-control and fulfillment in life. Only now one book at a promotional price of $100, and two - for the price of three. Kidding. I'd rather eat a kilo of licorice, which I hate, than be naïve enough to delude myself that there is one reliable way to live for everyone, and also to sell this bullshit to other people.

Human lives are very different, you know? When you bake a cake, you use virtually the same flour, water, and baking powder that every other person who baked that cake before you has used. Therefore, when you repeat all the steps from the recipe given by this man with one hundred percent accuracy (which is impossible in practice, because perhaps your oven will deceive you and does not really maintain a temperature of 180 degrees Celsius, but only 179.9 degrees), you can expect to end up with a practically identical cake. But if we want to transfer such a mechanism to human lives – we know that it will not work. You can't just copy someone else's steps and delude yourself that you will reach the same goal the same way. Everyone has a different psyche, a different body, different genes, different relationships and a different start, so everyone's path is truly unique. Yes, I know, it's a cliché. But again – how overlooked! How underestimated. Like all clichés. We are all completely different, although we tend to be guided by similar mechanisms. We all feel hungry, but one of us prefers to satisfy it with a sandwich with hummus and tomato, and another – with a giant burger and a portion of enlarged fries. Everyone feels the need for closeness, but someone can create a good relationship because of it, and someone else can complain that WOMEN/MEN are weird now, so he/she will never be able to find the right person.

Although we have similar needs, such as the need for sleep, food, security, self-fulfillment and maintaining good relationships with others, each of us feels them in a different intensity, in our own individual way. And each of us finds a different way to achieve them and has other opportunities in life that are conducive or not. Uncle Czesław can drive a rusty Opel because he loves this car and doesn't give a shit about what others think of it, and Uncle Stasio drives a new BMW on lease and laughs at his brother. Is it right? Of course rightly so! Who would want to drive an Opel there?!

Of course, this is a joke. No one should tell anyone that their choices are wrong UNLESS those choices cause someone else harm and suffering.

Czesław has the right, and maybe even the duty, to tell Stasio that kicking a dog is not okay, and although Stasio may be offended by it, Czesław is right. Czesław can admonish his brother that drinking alcohol every day threatens addiction and Stasio will probably also feel offended, but again, Czesio is right. In such cases, the criticism is justified and beneficial. But when it comes to personal tastes and preferences that don't affect anyone but the person who chooses them (for example, whether to have blonde hair or blue hair, or whether to build a house out of brick or wood), I think people might sometimes refrain from unnecessary criticism. However, am I not a hypocrite myself, criticizing criticism at this point? Absolutely! How!

There are no two identical cases, two identical people, no two identical stories. No two monkeys are alike. There are not even two identical bananas, because one could grow a millisecond longer and produce 0.0001 g of sugar less, or take 0.0001 g of potassium more, which of course our senses will not sense, but still – they are two different bananas. And you will never feel them in the same way, because the hydration of your mouth, sensitivity to dopamine or the sensitivity of the senses of taste and smell are changing all the time. Even atmospheric pressure affects the taste of a banana. How much you focus when eating fruit will never be the same either, because it depends on hundreds of biochemical processes taking place throughout your body, especially in the brain. All you have to do is sleep a few minutes less on a given day and your body will produce 0.01% less GABA, dopamine, acetylcholine or serotonin, and your appetite and ability to register sensory impressions will change slightly. It is enough that yesterday you ate a gram of olive oil more, and 1 g of butter less, for your ability to conduct nerve impulses to improve by, let's say, 0.001%, because olive oil contains omega-9 fatty acids, which build the myelin sheath of nerves, which improves impulse conduction. Every single experience you have is completely new and unique. So how do we know what the recipe for happiness is for all people? We have no idea. We don't even know what the recipe for happiness for an individual is. We can only guess and try as many things as we can to be able to more or less assess what works for us and what doesn't.

But if some desperate person threatened to cut all my hair if I didn't give him at least some hint as to where the recipe for a good life might lie, I'd tell him that building a good life and a happy psyche is a bit like building a house—you have to do it with a lot of small, different pieces. A house is not only made of bricks. There are also various cables, pipes, metal elements, wood here and there, and so on. In the same way, your life cannot be full if you do not include many different elements that interact and complement each other, right? Such elements can be, for example, self-control, empathy, good relationships with others, skilful financial management, a sense of inner peace, taking care of healthy sleep and diet, having goals and dreams, or personal development. If you don't have one of these, you may feel an indefinable feeling of emptiness or lack of fulfillment. You may have a worse and worse mood and performance, which will affect all the rest of your life. That's why, if I improve anything in myself, I try to approach it comprehensively – you can't just delude yourself that tomorrow you will start eating healthy and your whole life will change by one hundred percent. It will change, perhaps even more than you think, as one good change leads to another, more and more significant one. But it will not happen suddenly, in one day. When you lack balance between the various components of life, it is a bit like making a cake using five kilograms of flour and only one glass of water. What's worse – sometimes you have no idea what exactly you're missing. You are like a gorilla in the fog, stubbornly looking for bananas – and it turns out that in the jungle where he is searching, bananas do not grow at all. There are a lot of oranges, which are also tasty, but the gorilla doesn't see them because he focuses too much on bananas. He is looking for yellow.

Before I started writing, I had this problem. I had no purpose, and all my dreams were in a bag with the inscription "Maybe one day...", hidden deep in the closet of my subconscious. I wondered – why is my life so boring? Why do I feel bad? Why am I not satisfied with myself? Why do I feel stress and pressure to do more, and at the same time I don't have the strength to do anything? And most importantly – is it supposed to be like that? Is that it? Is this what my life will look like until the last days? Damn, a little weak.

Maybe some of you are asking yourself these questions too. Or maybe you asked yourself questions but stopped because they caused discomfort? Maybe you buried it under the carpet, hid it behind a closet, or threw it in the basement, like a banana peel, which you can bury in the ground and make something grow out of it? Or maybe you have just reached the point in your life where you can honestly say that you don't have to change anything anymore and you are completely happy? If so, congratulations.

However, for many years I was stuck in a place where my own psyche was my worst enemy, because something deeply did not fit me in life and what it looked like, and yet I had no idea what it was.

And what did I do? I decided to build a new, better me, brick by brick. Again, this sounds almost like the speech of cheesy motivational speakers, or like the talk of a jock who tells you the story of his life before he finally asks you for money, but unfortunately, or fortunately – that's the truth. If you want to change the overall way you feel, treat yourself like a beautiful home.

If you wanted to build a house, I bet you wouldn't hire a professional who claims to do it in two days. It's physically impossible, and if someone thinks they will do it – they would have to be a moron, or neglect the quality of this house to make it in time. Unless we are talking about a house built of ready-made prefabricated elements to be assembled, but there are no such elements in life.

First, I looked at my body, because it was the most obvious element that I could change. I went to the gym for a few years and had the basics of how to do it. However, when I stopped feeling the need to constantly improve my body, because I entered into a permanent relationship and felt that someone loved me regardless of whether I weighed 90 or 105 kilograms, I neglected my outer shell a bit.

Less muscle, more fat here and there, so it's probably logical that if I lose this fat and feel like a young god in my body again, I will regain the happiness that I have been missing for some time? Well, not exactly. But I deluded myself.

Have you noticed that people like to delude themselves? When we play gambling games with a very, very small chance of winning, we don't just buy a lottery ticket – we buy the hope that maybe our lives will change completely because we win this money. We pay to have at least a shadow of this hope for a better life. We buy vision. And this vision was created, of course, by someone who has a profit in it.

I'm not a patient person. I haven't written any of my books for more than three weeks, because I'm always in a hurry to publish them. I have strange, paranoid thoughts that if I die while writing, for example, because a piece of gold weighing five kilograms falls on me from the sky, all this work will be in vain. I had the same with weight loss – if you do it, do it as soon as possible!

So I followed a diet consisting only of fruits and nuts for a week and lost 3.5 kilograms, of which only a kilogram came back to me. It was probably the water I lost because I ate a lot less salt (which allows you to retain water in your body).

I also did the keto diet, the liquid diet, the English diet, the cigarette diet (I ate what I wanted, but I smoked more cigarettes to have less appetite – super smart approach!), the Mediterranean diet, or the vegetable diet?

On each of them you lose weight quite quickly, which of course was my main goal. And what are the disadvantages? After each of them, the kilograms come back very quickly.

Habits are built over weeks, and these diets cannot be followed for so long, because we would simply develop some deficiencies. The irony is that I work as a dietician and I am aware that the best eating styles are those that can stay with us for a long time, because when something becomes a habit, we don't even have to think about actually using it. We do this automatically. And when you start eating healthy or eating less, not because you force yourself, but because that's just your habit – it's really easy.

So when one of my patients told me that she would like to eat the most restrictive diet possible because she needs to lose 10 pounds in two months, I asked her – if you were to climb Mount Everest, which path would you choose? Fast, but very steep and dangerous, or a bit slower, but reliable and safe?

She answered: Fast!

And I said to her:

"So you fell. The fast way is not always the best.

As they say – you can quickly. But I didn't tell her that, of course, although she had a great sense of humor and a casual style of expression, so this joke would probably make her laugh.

I explained to her that the easiest ways are basically the best when it comes to building new habits, because difficult things make us quickly feel reluctant, tired, lose motivation and finally give up. And easy things – they're easy! Therefore, they are feasible.

If you had to eat a hundred bananas in one day, you'd sooner get diarrhea than complete the challenge. But eating a hundred bananas in a month sounds easy, doesn't it?

Another great irony of my life is that I'm great at giving advice to others, but it can take some time before I apply it myself. I assume that some people are smarter than me, or have more self-discipline, or just – somehow a given advice may be easier for them to apply than for me.

People can't just put every theory into practice at once. Knowledge is like a seed – if you have one, after some time, under favorable conditions, something can grow from it. But it doesn't have to be today. If someone uses at least one piece of advice contained in this book, gets inspired by at least one sentence, or becomes at least 1% wiser – that's already a success. I convey as much inspiration as possible, but I don't expect the reader to suddenly change 180 degrees as soon as they somehow get to the last sentence of my lyrical excerpts.

I like to collect knowledge and then spread it, but sometimes I'm just too lazy to use it. And that's okay. We are only human. That's a great excuse to do nothing, right?

Kidding! This is the purest obviousness. Life, the conditions in which we grew up, or the conditions in which we live now, have never been and will never be ideal. So why should we be? However, we can use the conditions in which we live as best we can. As long as we have the so-called motivation. That is, the first spark that ignites our enthusiasm to do something.

For example, when I stood in front of the mirror and saw a few kilograms of unnecessary fat on my belly... Do you think that was the spark for me? No. I ignored this fat. Who cares?

But when I tried to run, and after three minutes my lungs almost fell out through my nose... Do you think that was the spark? No. I just came home and found that I hated running.

But when we went to the beach and I saw that my friend had the perfect six-pack and he looked like he couldn't see life outside the gym... Do you think that was the spark? Neither. I thought, okay, maybe he has a nicer body, but he's a lot dumber. Phi, he certainly never wrote a single page of a book in his life. What a fool. Phi. I am simply focused on the development of the intellect, I don't have to have a perfect body.

But then I saw a video of someone running until they see a yellow car. And he ran, ran, ran... quite a long time. Of course, the pace of the recording was sped up about 10 times, which gave a spectacular effect in the form of a lot of changing landscapes that this runner passed. And then a spark appeared in my head, after all, running is so... freedom! When you run, you are not, like most people, only in one place. Your body carries you to different places. It's a completely different feeling than, for example, driving a car, where you also go to different places, but you don't get there on your own, you are dependent on the machine. Being able to run for a long time means in practice being devoid of the limits of your own body. So... Damn, I want to run!

And I started. Of course, I had to take a break after a maximum of three minutes each time, but as I lost weight (and reduced the number of pipes I smoked in a day), it became easier and easier. And finally I changed my attitude to running – I liked it. It has become a good way for me to overcome my own weaknesses and the limitations of my body, although it is still hellishly heavy.

Later, I started intermittent fasting (also known as the IF diet), which consists of skipping breakfast, for example. So I usually ate my first meal after work, that is, at 4 or 5 p.m. Of course, it's always something big and caloric, so you might think this diet is pointless, but if you manage to try it, you'll see how much potential it has. You burn fat for the first hours of the day, and then, even if you regain it, because you eat something that has even more calories than breakfast would have with dinner, you will gradually learn to control your hunger. And this is the most important thing. Then you will no longer eat such large portions in the evening, so you will start losing weight systematically.

Your insulin metabolism improves and your body learns to burn fat more efficiently. After just a few weeks, you stop feeling hungry in the morning, so this style of eating is not as torturous as it might seem. It becomes a habit easily, as long as you last the first month. And you don't have to do it as abruptly as I do. You can start eating at 12:00 instead of 7:00 if you have always been in the habit of eating breakfast. Then, once you get used to it, simply gradually move the time of your first meal forward.

You can also add two tablespoons of olive oil to your first meal, which is like the food of the gods. Although it has a lot of calories, it has been shown that people who added it to their meals ate 120 kcal less per day than people who did not. This is because olive oil helps to use up one's own fat reserves. So your body doesn't feel as hungry as it would if you didn't use oil.

In a word – everyone's body is a bit like a nook and cranny. Add a little olive oil to it and maybe it will just improve? It is not without reason that it is said that a healthy mind in a healthy body, oh not without reason! Inflammation in the body also means inflammation in the brain, and this increases the risk of depression. So when I was threatened by depression, or even when I already had it, I only denied it and deluded myself that it would go away on its own, at some point I realized that I was what I ate. If I want a healthier brain, I'll start eating healthier. And of course, it's better to start treating depression by changing your beliefs and mind than changing your diet, but if you combine these two methods, maybe it will work even better? Healthy thinking motivates you to be active and look for reasons to be happy, while a healthy diet enables physical support for the brain and greater production of serotonin or BDNF1. So maybe depression, as a rather complicated disease, requires treatment from two sides, just like a car that has various systems blown up, requires not only a change of brake pads, but also oil and gearbox? Look at life comprehensively and you will see more.

Exercise 31 – List 5 situations where easy solutions turn out to be much more effective than complicated ones.

Chapter 14: The Good

"If someone wishes you bad, you wish them well. Everyone gives to others what they have" – a beautiful quote. He literally blew my head because he made me realize that what you say and feel about others also affects you. So in order to get out of mental lows, sometimes it is worth starting by looking at others as you would like others to look at you. Wishing and doing what you would like to be done and wished for you. Because when you wish others bad, you're actually convincing your brain that life is bad and people are bad, so they deserve evil. When you learn to forgive them and wish them well despite their flaws – your mind benefits from it, because it begins to believe that people deserve good.

A Pole, a Frenchman, a German and an Italian caught a goldfish. And of course, she spoke to them in a human voice:

-If you are good enough to give me life, I will make one wish for each of you!

So the German began without hesitation:

"You know what? I have one dream! My neighbor has a wonderful villa with a swimming pool, he is the president of a large corporation, he drives a Ferrari. He achieves great financial successes. And me? They fired me from my job because I was too lazy! I don't have my own house or car. Please make me rich too! I can't look at my neighbor and endure the sick jealousy that eats me away. My nation values diligence and reliability very much, and I failed in this field. Make me a successful man, please!

-Poof! Wish granted! Next please!

Then the Italian spoke:

-You know what, goldfish? My neighbor is a famous chef, he can cook really well! And me? I can't even get jam on a slice of bread properly, let alone make Bruscetta, speghetti or Lasagna... Please improve my cooking skills so that I can be a famous chef too! As you probably know, my nation values good food, and I feel that I'm not even average in this field. This is my biggest complex, because otherwise I have a pretty good life.

-Poof! Done. From now on, you are an outstanding chef. Next!

The Frenchman said:

- My neighbor is a connoisseur of art. Every day she sees beauty and surrounds herself with beauty. He has a gallery with paintings by famous artists, where he spends a lot of time. He has a vineyard with the best wines, which he drinks with delight. He listens to wonderful, classical music, his wife is beautiful, his children are beautiful. He writes poems, financially supports beginner writers, poets and painters. As you probably know, my nation appreciates romance and beauty. That is why I cannot look at him without painful jealousy, knowing that I have nothing beautiful and am not so sensitive to beauty! My soul is petrified and sad. Make my life beautiful too!

-Poof! Done. And you, what do you want, Pole?- asked the fish.

- I am a farmer. However, I only have one hectare of field. And my neighbor? It has ten hectares. What's worse – she has a herd of beautiful cows. Over 300 wonderful specimens! I can't look at it!

- What, you just want more cows and a field? - asked the fish, slightly surprised by the simplicity of this wish, but still full of appreciation for the farmer, who apparently loves what he does, so he wants to be better at it...

-No! Make my neighbor's cows die!- the Pole replied and laughed diabolically.

Of course, this is just a joke. I do not intend to spread stereotypes or criticize my own nation, but only to demonstrate what envy looks like in practice. I don't want to generalize and pigeonhole people, but I admit that often, we Poles have many advantages, they are really important – we are hardworking, we are very persistent, and as a rule, we try to keep our word, because words are important to us. However, we have one small flaw – envy.

If you are a Pole, like me, don't feel offended by reading this. If the problem of jealousy or envy does not concern you – great, congratulations. However, if you felt offended – well, maybe it's worth thinking about it a bit? Why do you feel offended at all if you don't have this problem? If you have it, force yourself to think of others well. Seriously, it's easy, because you can choose what you think. You won't get rid of negativity overnight, but thinking at least 1% better every day, after a year you will feel a big difference, believe me.

Sometimes, when I feel like "unwinding" myself a bit (each of us needs it, it's normal. You can't function healthily using 100 percent of your intellectual abilities all the time and think about everything, everywhere, always), I browse short videos on Facebook, Instagram or YouTube. Unfortunately, it doesn't give the expected result of relaxation and brainwashing, because I tend to read the comments under these videos. For example:

- The film shows the pros and cons of Tesla (the car, not the famous inventor). Someone just wanted to boast that they have a Tesla, and describe the pros and cons of this car honestly. And that's okay. Ration?

According to the commenters – unfortunately not. Most often I see comments like:

"This electric shit will never go as far as a gasoline car anyway!

-I'm waiting impatiently for this Tesla to burn you down!

-Do you think it's ecological?! Wrong! Button, right! Ecology is stupid propaganda and you fell for it!

-A pile of scrap metal! I prefer my old Passat! I would never buy a Tesla in my life!

In another video, a chubby girl shows off her diet, which she uses to lose a few pounds. It is supposed to be motivating and inspiring, and show that you don't have to eat some fancy products or count calories restrictively to lose weight. As for me - a great initiative! Certainly better than the so-called Mukbang, i.e. films in which someone eats huge amounts of food, often unhealthy. So I'm going into the comments with the intention of writing to this girl that she's great, beautiful and doing a good job. And what did others write?

- You fat pig, you won't lose weight by eating such unhealthy products!

-You eat practically only sugar! Where's the fat?! Fat should be the basis of your diet! Keto beyond life!

- Wrong! Not enough protein! Eat more protein!

-Fu, disgusting! How can you brag about having such an ugly body and such a horrible diet! Shame on you!

Sure, there were also nice comments, but there was a reason why the negative ones were at the very top and had the most likes. When people feel unpunished and anonymous (and this is the possibility, although this is a false assumption, is given to them by the Internet), they are simply mean to themselves. And they like to make fun of other people and their weaknesses. It's terrible.

I'm not the nicest person in the world. I can also be mean, often in a very painful, hurtful, cynical and rude way – but only for people who are mean or socially harmful themselves and "deserve" it. If I see that someone is trying to do something good, motivate or inspire people – I always try to be nice to such a person.

Why?

Because why not?

What would the world look like if we abandoned all negativity for just a year and simply wished other people well, supported them, wanted the best for them? How much better would life be for all of us?

When you see a newborn trying to take his first steps, but falls over every now and then, what do you think about?

- Hmm, stupid newborn, he can't even walk! Ha ha ha! I'm so better than him!

Do you think that way? I don't think so. That would be stupid.

If it's your child, or the child of someone you know, you may even want to help them take their first steps and support their effort by giving them a hand so that they can first learn to walk with your little support and then on their own. And this is beautiful. Maybe each of us has a bit of empathy? It would be nice to live in a world where this empathy is not limited to children.

So why can't many of us support adults in this way?

Why, when someone tries to do something, an envious compatriot says:

-Don't even try, loser! You won't make it! You are naïve to believe that you will ever achieve anything! Phi, when I was your age, I did it twice as well! You don't have a talent for it, let it go!

Instead of:

- It's nice that you're trying! I admire it! I respect that! You keep going! Maybe you're making mistakes for now, maybe this or that thing needs to be corrected, but you're trying, and that's important! If you really want to be good at it, exercise regularly and you will!

It is said that a Pole is a wolf to a Pole (and kiwi kiwi kiwi). In a world full of wolves, however, there is a fight for dominance, a struggle for who has a bigger ego and a better life, who is stronger, richer and wiser. Maybe, as I mentioned at the very beginning, we are all in the same boat, we play in the same team, to the same goal, because each of us has his own personal contribution to society? So maybe it's worth supporting each other, because the world without a fight will be better? Do you prefer to live in a world of war, hatred and fear, or in a safe and empathetic one? I assume that in the second, so although it is not easy, it is worth using small manifestations of empathy and goodness every day, because everything starts with small steps, and every small change in society by 1% per year will make society better by 270% after 100 years (the magic of compound interest).

Let's just think for a moment about what we expect from life. Most likely – everything that is good. Ba! All the best! Because of course we deserve it, am I right? But is it possible to get something for free? Would it be logical and just if you suddenly, from an unknown source, began to receive all blessings from life, even though you yourself cannot give these blessings to others? Consider. Throw this book in the trash... Kidding! Don't do it. Take it out of the basket, but set it aside for a while. Think for one, two, or maybe even ten minutes – what can you give to others? And how much do you actually give? And then think also – how much do you expect from others? And how much do you actually get?

Today, a good friend of mine boasted that he made just over $1,000 in crypto in a few days by investing around $15,000. Its results and profits are constant, almost daily. His investment strategy is apparently outstanding, as the value of his portfolio has been growing for weeks.

Did I feel a pang of jealousy when I found out? No. Not even the slightest trace of jealousy. This news made my morning better, because I think my friend is hellishly intelligent and at the same time a good-hearted man, so he completely deserves it. I rejoiced in his happiness, sincerely and completely.

Although I have been interested in investing myself for many years (but not in crypto, but in stocks), I have never had a daily profit of more than $100, and the amount of losses I have incurred by mindlessly testing various investment strategies far exceeds the amount of my profits so far. I have very high expectations of myself, high ambitions and the belief that intelligent people should be able to make money on the stock market, and yet – so far I can't do it. So I would have a perfect reason to feel inferior to my friend and suffer a serious damage to my ego. However, this did not happen. Why? Because I definitely wish him the best.

Yes, if someone else was doing so well, I'd probably feel a pang of unhealthy jealousy, but I'd still try to understand my feelings and explain to myself that if this person is apparently better at it than me, they probably have a better strategy, a more composed psyche, or a higher IQ, so they deserved it. Not everyone who earns a lot of money fully deserves it and is a good person – there is no doubt about it. There are people who spend their fortune on yachts, private jets, giant villas or champagne and cocaine, and zero on charitable foundations, planting forests or helping other people. Yes, it's sad. But still, I'd rather feel nothing for such people than feel toxic jealousy or envy.

When I wake up in the morning and see someone driving a brand new Porshe, and I'm traveling to work by bus, I don't have thoughts like:

-One hundred percent this man earned a fortune from the harm of others! He probably pays his employees pennies, and he reaps most of the profits from his company. Or he cheats people by selling them magic stones and making them believe that they will solve their problems! Or robbed a bank! Or he robs old ladies by hacking into their bank accounts with viruses sent through suspicious links in SMS.

No. That would not only be a stupid and harmful assumption, but above all a great blockade for my mind from achieving anything in the financial field in the future. If you believe that every rich person is bad and that the only way to make money is to hurt others, you will never become rich, because you prefer to be a good person, and these two situations are mutually exclusive in your mind.

However, when you understand that entrepreneurs and their employees are often put in a "win-win" situation, where everyone wins because they both have some benefits from their cooperation, you give yourself permission to feel happiness from something that would seem obvious – cooperation with another person. Other people don't feel that happiness because instead of focusing on their own profit and appreciating it, they focus on the fact that their boss has even more profit. And they envy him.

When I go to work, I try to do everything the best I can. I respect my boss and I am full of admiration for him, because he built a great company from scratch, only thanks to hard work and high intelligence. Although many things could look better in my current company, I still have gratitude in my mind that I have this job, because... I might not have had it. Simple. My job is a win-win-win-win situation, where I win – because I earn, the boss wins – because he earns, our partners win – because they earn, and the end customers win because they have the products they wanted, delivered to them by our partners.

Life shouldn't be about slavery, because everyone wants to be free, right? But you don't have to be locked in a cage to be a slave. Often, the only form of slavery a person has is his own beliefs. That's why I'm amused by comments from people who complain about their work every day, saying that they feel like slaves in it, or that capitalism is a modern form of enslavement, and all the big companies are just out to us up and make us obedient, stupid slaves.

Or maybe the world just works in this unpleasant way only when you think it works that way?

I think that a company that produces sweet, unhealthy jelly beans doesn't force them into my mouth. They did not chain me to a tree and say to me:

-Hey, stupid! From now on, you are to buy our jelly beans every week and eat them with a smile on your face!

No.

I, of my own free will, buy jelly beans from this one particular company, because they are incredibly good and have 50% fruit juice, which gives them an outstanding taste compared to other gummies. I'm not a slave to sugar. I may not eat it for days and I hate it. But I like jelly beans, and someone else makes good jelly beans. Win-win. I don't have to have a perfect diet 24/7 to live a healthy life.

I wish the best to this one particular company that produces relatively healthy, tasty, ethical jelly beans. There are also companies that I don't wish well, because, for example, they buy cocoa from farms where children are slaved. But it is me who chooses which of these companies I will give money, and therefore which of them I want to work with. It's simple.

Everywhere, always, every time – life is about your attitude. If you want to feel good, you must first of all start with a good attitude towards the things that surround you. And to people too. If you wish ill to others, you look for enemies, conspiracies and threats everywhere – it is rather unlikely that you will ever experience full happiness. However, if you even try to shift your mindset to appreciating others and wishing them the best, you may find that it's actually pleasurable and soothing to the mind. Because you have it in you! You have good. You just have to get them out. And once you start thinking of other people in a good way, it can be a great first step. I know it sounds trivial, but think about it – isn't our life made up of such small, everyday clichés, which when added up add up to something bigger? Every little thought, emotion, habit – after many days, if you repeat them regularly, they will become part of your personality.

On the one hand, what matters in life is simply and above all the desire to do good, i.e. good character. On the other hand, someone who said that money does not bring happiness was probably an idiot. Someone who has money can create up to a thousand jobs for others. Someone who does not have them, unfortunately, cannot. Ideally, a person should be both good, so he had the desire to change the world for the better, and rich, so he had the opportunity to do so. However, as we know, life is not perfect, and rich people are sometimes dicks devoid of empathy (but not all of them).

Fortunately, even the poorest person can, of course, do good on a small scale, and it would be very nice if every average person did it. When you do good, you feel good yourself. So when you have no purpose in life and no hope for a better tomorrow (there is always hope, but maybe you don't see it today), instead of focusing on self-destruction and scratching your mental wounds, find some escape and relief in helping others? Maybe it will make your life meaningful and purposeful?

I recommend, encourage, persuade. The point is that doing good makes us believe that we are needed by someone, so yes, life, although hard, makes sense. We make a real contribution to society. We, poor people, of course, CAN do as much good as possible, but this is not a competition of "who will give more", so since we all serve the same purpose, let's not race, and let everyone contribute as much as they can. In my case, altruistic behavior greatly improved my mood when I needed it most, so I recommend this way to support the treatment of depression. We, the poor, also have an impact on the world, and if it is good – karma comes back. Dog food? No. That good energy.

Final Words:

It would be impossible to include all the information about depression in such a short book, so it is (like any other book) a more or less generalized collection of what I know, what I understand and what I consider important.

Depression is a really poorly understood and complex disease, so it is worth getting to know it better and reading more books, especially scientific ones, written by specialists.

However, it is also worth reading books that are generally thought-provoking, containing thoughts on the nature of the human mind, because perhaps in them you will find something that will work on and tell you what is worth working on in your case to feel better

Each chapter of this book discusses a different perspective and approach that is worth having in order to think healthily and positively, which will certainly contribute to faster treatment of depression, but GOD FORBID YOU to abandon the therapy recommended by a psychologist, because this is the main healing tool, the best we have at the moment. Let books, change of thinking and work on habits be a nice, beneficial, but still only addition.

If you had a friend who tells you every day that you're bad person, would you be satisfied with such a relationship? If he clipped your wings again and again, convincing you that you will never achieve anything, Your life has no meaning, you are ugly and others are doing much better in life, would you blossom mentally with such a person? Or maybe you'd get fed up with the bastard and tell him to shut up?

Now look at the internal dialogue. The way that your own brain talks with you. Does this jelly give you beneficial and valuable thoughts, or is he like a mean friend? In fact, You are in control of your brain and what you think about. But Your brain in some way controls you too. You fight with each other, like two monkeys for the last banana. And life doesn't have to be about fighting. Knowing how a monkey thinks and acts will allow you to tame it and make friends with it, just as knowing how the brain, mind and emotions work can make you tame this brilliant machine and instead of falling to its negative influences, make it generate pleasant, positive thoughts for you. Make Your brain Your friend, not enemy. That's all.

If you are not aware of your thoughts, they come out of your brain automatically, like the spoiled kebab you ate yesterday, coming out of your body's exhaust pipe under high pressure. However, when you catch yourself thinking about something, you can stop the negative thought at any time and say to yourself – why am I thinking about such stupid things? This is not true, but only my opinion. And the opinion can always be changed. Habits too. Emotions too. You just have to learn how to control your mind. A pilot learns to fly for many months until filally being able to fly himself, so why wouldn't we learn to use our own brains? God damn! I am sure that Your brain is even more complicated than an airplane, so it's worth learning how to use it! Although it's not easy and takes time – I think that each of us will benefit from learning it, because after all, what you have in your head – this jelly with billions of neurons – is you.

That's all for now. Take control and be friends with Your jelly.

If the subject of the human psyche interests you, and you also resonate in some way with my thoughts, I encourage you to read my other book – „Focus" that You can get at Amazon. And if you want a sarcastic SF story describing human stupidity, I recommend "Me Be Only Monkey" ☺

Thank you for your time

And I wish you that this reading will result in a good change!

Damian Podpora

Printed in Dunstable, United Kingdom